after the rip.

Copyright © 2020 by Kimberly Elaine Adams

All rights reserved.

No part of this book may be reproduced in any form or by any electronic or mechanical means, including information storage and retrieval systems, without written permission from the author, except for the use of brief quotations in a book review.

ISBN: 978-1-7344813-0-3

Printed in USA

❦ Created with Vellum

after the rip.

BY

AUTHOR

KIMBERLY ELAINE ADAMS

*This book is dedicated to the millions of singles that married but did not get to experience the "happily ever after."
There is LIFE after...*

CONTENTS

Acknowledgments ix
Foreword xiii
Introduction xvii

CHAPTER 1 - FIGURING ME OUT — 1
CHAPTER 2 - WHY DID I GET MARRIED? — 12
CHAPTER 3 - I's MARRIED NOW! — 18
CHAPTER 4 - THE TRAUMA NAMED DIVORCE! — 29
CHAPTER 5 - THE GRIEVING PROCESS! — 37
CHAPTER 6 - MAKING THE DECISION TO FORGIVE — 47
CHAPTER 7 - JOURNALING — 63
CHAPTER 8 - DENOUNCING the SPIRIT of REJECTION — 67
CHAPTER 9 - CONCENTRATING on ME and My Future — 80
CHAPTER 10 - CONTINUE HEALING and DELIVERANCE — 89
About the Author — 100

Acknowledgments

I would like to thank my Lord and Savior Jesus Christ for saving me, delivering me and setting me free!

Never in a million years, after my divorce, did I ever think God would use it or me to write a book about the process. Although this book is geared toward the divorced and divorcing, it is not limited to that particular demographic.

This is a book about life, its joys and disappointments and how to recover despite the crippling emotional trauma that's been experienced. Rips are caused by many circumstances and occur through various experiences. Rips happen every day to every person of every race, creed, nationality and religious and spiritual denomination. No one is immune and every human being is vulnerable. For this reason, this book is for everyone that has ever had to recover from any trauma in their life.

I thank God for my parents, **William Charles Adams, Jr. and Jacqueline McMullen Adams** for loving each other and creating me as a result. This book is a result of their union and was released on their ***55th Wedding Anniversary, June 21, 2020.***

I am a particularly blessed woman to have had, known and loved but most of all been loved by two sets of grandparents… the **Late Williams Charles Adams, Sr. and the Late Rossie Lee Barnes Adams** (paternal grandparents) and (maternal grandparents) the **Late**

Willie E. McMullen, Sr. and my 97 year young grandmother **Hettie Hall McMullen.**

My life is filled with love from my siblings: **Valleri Adams, William Adams, Michael Adams** and the **Late Jason Adams** who will forever be remembered with the greatest love! I thank God for them being my greatest supporters and cheerleaders!

Without these three human beings I would not know the depth of LOVE and sacrifice. They are manifestations of my heart walking around in human form in the earth, my sons **Toreon, Tavin and Robert.**

I thank God for my precious grandchildren who God sent to change the trajectory of our lives.

I honor my Godmothers who are no longer with me on earth but are among the heavenly witnesses. They were my prayer warriors, exhorters, encouragers and on so many days gave me words of wisdom and supernatural strength. I would not be who I am today without them on this journey: *Mother Essie Cunningham* and *Mother Mary Woods.*

And finally, to my spiritual father **Apostle Travis C. Jennings** and my spiritual mother **Pastor Stephanie L. Jennings**, I say "Thank You" for all of the years of prophecies, counsel, teaching, examples, love, respect and correction. This book is now in the earth's realm because you birthed it out of me. I am forever humbled, honored and grateful to represent a *Seal of your Apostleship* and to serve under your leadership at the greatest church on this side of heaven - **The Harvest Tabernacle Church!**

Lord, I thank you for every person reading the pages of this book. May it bring revelation, healing and deliverance. Lord, I ask you to touch the heart that has been hurt and life that has been devastated by this tragedy. I thank you that they will find peace and solace in the words written and that their lives will be transformed to exemplify the love of Christ manifested in the earth.
In Jesus' Name!

Edited by Ayanna Kilgore

Book cover by Eric Byrd

Scriptures taken from the Holy Bible, New International Version®, NIV®. Copyright © 1973, 1978, 1984, 2011 by Biblica, Inc.™ Used by permission of Zondervan. All rights reserved worldwide. www.zondervan.com The "NIV" and "New International Version" are trademarks registered in the United States Patent and Trademark Office by Biblica, Inc.®

Scriptures marked KJV are taken from the KING JAMES VERSION (KJV): KING JAMES VERSION, public domain.

FOREWORD

Marriage statistics currently report that almost 50% of all marriages in the United States will end in divorce or separation. Researchers estimate that 41% of all first marriages end in divorce, and 60% of second marriages end in divorce. Lastly, researchers report that 73% of all third marriages end in divorce. The United States has the 6th highest divorce rate in the world.

These are startling statistics about an institution sanctioned by God. This manuscript isn't about how to combat these stats or how to "fireproof" your marriage so that it can last. No, it doesn't include tricks and tips on how to take your "marriage to the max" or how to keep the "sizzle" in your marriage sizzling, there are plenty of *Vogue* or *Cosmopolitan* articles and books that lists practical steps, and explanations, on these common marital topics. **This is not that.** However, Kimberly Adams felt the burden to address the other side of these alarming statistics—the other 40% to 50% of people who move on after divorce. Though divorce is considered a "death," Kimberly Adams lovingly outlines, and effectively proves that there is indeed, *life after divorce,* in her authoring debut, **after the rip.**

Webster defines a rip as a long tear or cut. Remarkably transparent, Adams invites the reader into the "tear" of her own life. With **after the rip**, Adams affectionately documents the real-life choice she has also made to live her own life to the fullest, and her intention to not leave anything for the grave. One thing she wants her readers to know, choosing to live is just that —**a choice.** Adams is a walking miracle, and her experience has transformed into wisdom for those who find themselves on the other side of these marital stats and are struggling with how to live a life—**after the rip.**

For the past 14 years, I've had the fortunate honor of pastoring Kimberly Adams. During this time, I've witnessed both her spiritual and natural matriculation. I've observed how she has successfully navigated certain trials in her life, while displaying an unwavering dedication to her family, and her Christ-like commitment to the people of God, while working in ministry. All of this while picking up the pieces of her life after her own divorce. She was vulnerable and she was true to her process. Minister Adams is an accomplished woman, full of grace who has traveled all over the world. Minister Kimberly Adams is *totally qualified* to minister to those who are broken in this area.

I believe that **after the rip** will serve as a mirror for

those who may find themselves on the other side of marriage. I believe that those that find themselves here will not view it as a death sentence, but they will see this place as an opportunity to pursue destiny—just as Adams has—after reading her manuscript. Many will see themselves through Adams' life. They will choose to live because of her example. They will reflect, they will become angry, they will laugh, they will cry—but they will live. I am proud to call Minister Kimber Adams, Daughter.

Apostle Travis C. Jennings, Author of:
The Gathering of Champions: It's time to Get in the Ring
Life on Turbo
Lifeguard: Help is On the Way
Faith for the Gold
Influencers
How to Love a Black Woman
www.theharvesttabernacle.org

INTRODUCTION

Why did I write this book? Why isn't church enough? The church has all the answers for a dying world. We have the word of God and we have the anointing of the Holy Ghost with the evidence of speaking in tongues. We have beautiful sanctuaries, edifices, community centers and world renown ministries...so why would we need instructions on how to be restored or healed from divorce when divorces should not be happening under the covering of the church?

This book exists because, unfortunately, divorce exists. The person trying to process through this strange jungle needs real strength, guidance and support.

Divorce can be described as a violent "RIPPING" of

INTRODUCTION

the marriage covenant. It is painful to every member of the immediate family as well as the extended family unit (in-laws, church family, friends, relatives, etc).

According to enrichment journal on the divorce rate in America the statistics are as follows:

The divorce rate in America for first marriage is 41%

The divorce rate in America for second marriage is 60%

The divorce rate in America for third marriage is 73%

And believe this or not, the group with the highest reported divorce rate are evangelical Christians.

Barna report: Variation in divorce rates among Christian faith groups:

Denomination (in order of decreasing divorce rate) % who have been divorced:

Non-denominational ** 34%

Baptists 29%

Mainline Protestants 25%

Mormons 24%

Catholics 21%

Lutherans 21%

George Barna, president and founder of the Barna Research Group, commented:

"While it may be alarming to discover that born again Christians are more likely than others to experience a divorce, that pattern has been in place for quite some time. Even more disturbing, perhaps, is that when those individuals experience a divorce, many of them feel their community of faith provides rejection rather than support and healing."

As you can see by the statistics, being "saved" or part of the local "Body of Christ" does not make us immune to the disease or dysfunction of divorce. As you can also see, a second or third marriage has less likelihood of success than a first marriage. This would imply that believing that you simply made the wrong choice in mates "the first time" is a false belief. The issue is much deeper than just choices.

Without the most devastating event that I have experienced to date, I would not be who I am today. I wouldn't be the confident, brilliant, intelligent, amazing teacher, minister, manager or woman of God that my process cultivated me into. The event that I am referring to is "Divorce". Surprised? Me too!

Twenty years ago when I was crying into my pillow every night for months and praying for God to touch my (ex) husband's heart and mind to come back to me, to us (our 3 sons) by any means necessary, I would never have imagined how important that process would be in forming an incredible new version of myself.

The process of divorce forced me to take a look at myself as I had never had to look at myself before. I had to take a look at me; the real me. The me that I didn't really want to see; the flawed me; the misguided me, the misunderstood me, the rejected me, the abandoned me, the selfish me, the unforgiving me.

Of course, I had a choice. I could take a look at me

INTRODUCTION

or I could continue to go on with life in the bubble that I had existed in for most of it. But clearly existing in that bubble wasn't getting me where I wanted to be. So, my choice was inevitable……take a look; a real look; a discerning look, an uncomfortable look, a scary look ……..at me. I made the choice to look within and made the decision that I would not faint or turn back no matter what I discovered.

How is it that you can live 35 years of life without ever really knowing who you are, how you've come to do what you do or think how you think? What's stranger is that you can live this way and never question yourself until something happens. Something significant happens. Something devastating happens. Something happens to provoke your thoughts, your curiosity and suddenly there is an overwhelming need to find the answer to all of the questions that you never even thought to ask. It's during these times that you find yourself questioning your life, it's purpose, your reality and even your entire existence.

So yes, I only started to ask these questions after I experienced my divorce. And thankfully my gracious Heavenly Father consoled me, healed me, delivered me and on top of it all answered all of my questions.

Unfortunately, we only have a limited number of pages for a book and cannot go through all of the reasons or causes of divorce. It varies from couple to couple, origin of the relationship, personalities, experiences and so on.

INTRODUCTION

What I can do is give you information and understanding of how you can successfully process and live your life healed, delivered and set free after this devastating event, this "ripping," has occurred.

CHAPTER 1 - FIGURING ME OUT

Who Am I?

In order for the Lord to answer my questions, I had to be open, honest and transparent with Him and myself. I had to be willing to confront situations that life had thrown at me along the way. This was the only way the question I had: "How have I come to the place where I do what I do and think the way that I think" could be answered.

There are a few defining moments in my life which have helped me understand who I am. Among these include my birth position in my family, my parents, my siblings, my formative years in elementary, middle and high school and my decision to join the US Army. This chapter answers the "Who Am I" questions.

My entire extended family knows that I usually introduce myself as the first child of five born to my parents and the first grandchild born on both sides of the family. What my family doesn't know is the reason I introduce myself that way. I've learned that the more you know about a person's foundation, their upbringing, life events and experiences, the more you can understand them. I've also learned that my birth position in life pre-determined a lot of my personality traits and characteristics. By giving this brief but important information, I have informed listeners that I have a foundation of love and significance. After all, who is more significant than the first born? The first born is the gateway to all others. The first born is just that, the first to get all of the time, attention, and as we read in the bible, "the blessings"! Because I was the first born, I had a great sense of entitlement that I recognized at an early age. I also had a voice. My parents, grandparents, aunts, uncles and every person associated with both families allowed me to talk and allowed me to be heard. I was very expressive as a young child and remember talking to adults a lot. As a matter of fact, I recall adults saying to me "you are awfully mature for your age. You must spend a lot of time around grown-ups." Even with these statements, they all continued in conversation with me. I don't ever recall being told to "shut up," "hush," or "be quiet!" It seemed that I was always talking to people who wanted to hear me talk.

My parents moved from our small hometown of Tuscaloosa, Alabama to Miami, Florida when I was around four years old. My younger sister was around two years old and my baby brother was an infant. We are all basically two years apart.

I remember my siblings being born and how my role started changing, but not my significance. I was still the first born and I still reigned. My next brother came two years later and by the time my parents gave birth to my last sibling, which was another baby brother, I had become a full-fledged surrogate mother at the age of eleven. Like many other children in my era, this surrogate role was not one that I asked for, wanted or was even qualified to have; it was a position I inherited out of sheer necessity.

My parents were young and alone raising a large family outside of their support system which was a few states away. Both of my parents worked, which meant my siblings and I were either in daycare, with care givers or being cared for by me. This caregiver role was not a full-time position. I was only put into that position when absolutely necessary and for short periods of time for an hour, 30 minutes or less. I would change my baby brother's diapers (fourth child), feed him, and made sure that my other siblings knew that I was in charge while my parents were not home. I became an expert tattletale. I ran a tight ship, which is probably the reason my parents knew they could entrust me with looking after my siblings. I followed all rules. I didn't question my parents about my responsibilities. I knew I was supposed to be obedient, good and smart, and so I was. Afterall, I wanted my parents to know that I was a good and loveable child. I never wanted to disappoint them.

Actually, none of this sounds so bad to me now. I only had to give up being a safety patrol officer and a few extra-curricular activities to assist my folks. When I think about it, I wasn't really giving them up because my parents couldn't afford them anyway.

So how was this a bad thing? Well, it was more a matter of not being a good thing because I became responsible for the lives and decisions of others, prematurely. I was barely able to make good decisions for myself; therefore, the responsibility of younger siblings was not a good position to be placed in so early in life.

This early responsibility planted a seed in me that I was responsible (at all times) for the decisions of others and that my livelihood was dependent on them making the right decisions. It also planted a seed of "control" in me very early in life. In order to get the results I felt I needed or deserved, I started policing others to do their part and make the right decisions. This assured that "we" as a unit, and specifically I, wouldn't get into trouble for them making bad decisions. This is a character trait that I have had to fight for years. I always seemed to know the right answer and the correct move and decision a person should make; therefore, I was always eager to share that information with them whether it was requested or not. Can you imagine a little human being not only guiding younger siblings but offering advice to older youth and even adults?

Well, here she was. This characteristic caused me to embrace **false burdens** – where usually there is a false guilt to help others or to cover up your own pain because of the spirit of rejection. Taking false responsibility for others.

In elementary school I had lots of accomplishments. I was a good reader, a fast runner, a natural dancer (ballet and modern) and talented in poetry and acting. All of these talents helped create a great sense of confidence.

Through my middle and high school years that confidence started to dwindle as I endured many unexpected life changes. After 6th grade, my family moved back to Tuscaloosa, Alabama, my parent's hometown and my birthplace. Our relatives were excited that we were back. Our extended family reached out to us with love and showered us with gifts the first Christmas that we were back. Though it was sweet finally being around my extended family, that time for me could only be described as awkward and uncomfortable. We moved from a very diverse community of Blacks, Whites, Cubans, Haitians, Puerto Ricans, etc. to "the deep south." In Alabama, I suddenly became a "race." There were only two races; two cultures; two ethnicities to be categorized as. You were simply either Black or White. Simple and sad!

My world was shattered. I didn't fit in to this new place. In Miami I felt as if I was a part of my community. I was accepted; I was somewhat special; I was okay. I was an excellent student, had stable friendships and pretty much enjoyed everyday life, even with the small inconveniences that I endured.

In addition to moving to Alabama the summer before my 13th birthday, my father decided to enroll me and my siblings into the "Minority to Majority" school program. Because schools were still segregated upon our return to Alabama, the only way to integrate them was through this busing program. Though my family lived on the west or Black side of town, my siblings and I were bused to the east or White side of town for school.

The school was predominately White (Caucasian). In this new world, I was constantly reminded that I was Black, now referred to as African-American. I was constantly looked upon as if I was inferior and I was constantly told by my teachers that I was behind schedule. I didn't measure up; I did not do well in 7th grade at all. My grades were average, my confidence began to shrink and suddenly I found myself to be an outsider. To add to those stresses, I was a late bloomer. I was built like a stick; not just a stick, a tall, skinny, shapeless stick. Why didn't I know that I didn't measure up when I lived in Miami? Why did my teachers lead me to believe that I was smart and beautiful? Why did they allow me to have so much confidence? It was only six months later and suddenly the world realized my lack of voluptuousness and wanted to ensure that I was aware of it at every opportunity. All the boys told me how "flat" I was daily. Hmmm, as if I could do anything about my body build.

Like most parents, my father tried to reassure me that there was nothing wrong with me. He kept telling me that I wasn't skinny and that I was just fine. Of course he thought I was just fine, he was my father. All fathers, or at least all parents, think that their kid is just fine. However, what parents can't do is un-convince you of what your entire world has convinced you of.

That year, I recall becoming good friends with a girl named Alice who just happened to be a white girl. She was not from Tuscaloosa either. As a matter of fact, she wasn't from the South at all. I don't remember if she was from the West Coast or East Coast, but I do remember that she had a "proper" accent. She definitely didn't sound like she was from the south. She was also very open to me as a friend; therefore, prejudice was not really a part of her demeanor. Alice invited me to her birthday party at the local skating rink. Her mom actually had a van and picked several kids up and took us to the rink. I don't think Alice or I realized that I would be the only Black friend at her party. I was so excited for the day of her birthday party. My mom bought a nice gift for me to give her. Unfortunately, Alice's new friends were not as accepting or tolerant of other races as she was. She found herself in a compromising position. She really couldn't give me much attention at her party because she had lots of other friends there to entertain. None of her new friends talked to me or played any skating games with me that day. I became pretty conscious and intimidated by the event after about 30 minutes. I knew that I couldn't go home until it was over, so I just made the best of it. I skated, I sat alone, I watched the group laugh and skate and I waited until it was over. At the end of the party, Alice's mom loaded us all into her van and we proceeded on the drive to drop me off first. On the drive to the west side, the Black side, my side of town, the kids made lots of jokes about the surroundings. They joked about things that I had never noticed before. They joked about the broken-down homes, the old broken-down cars and the men and kids walking around in what appeared to them as rags. They even joked that my side of town was only for monkeys. They never spoke directly to me, just out loud. They laughed and everyone, including my friend Alice, laughed too. It was impossible for Alice's mom not to hear the ugliness displayed in the van; but she just chose to ignore it. The only correction I recall her giving was that they were too loud, and she had to concentrate on driving. Maybe she felt the same way all of the mean little white kids felt. At one point, my feelings were so hurt that I got confused and lost track of where I was. This was long before GPSs or map apps. Alice's mom was asking me which street I lived on and I couldn't clearly remember. My heart was racing, I felt a great sense of anxiety and of course the mean white kids had to pick at me about that as well. "What dumb ____ doesn't know where they live?" Then they laughed uncontrollably. Alice's mom grew impatient with me. I apologized, but suddenly recognized where I was. Whew, I pointed. "There, turn right there. My house is on the left". I got out of the van, thanked Alice's mom for dropping me at home. The laughter was as strong as ever as I walked up the driveway of my grandparent's house on 23rd Street. My grandparent's house was the best, most beautiful, brick house on the entire street. My grandparent's never locked their doors. The house was open to pretty much everyone that decided to pay them a visit (drunks, drug addicts and all). I walked into the house and immediately headed to my room, laid on my bed and cried. At that moment I absolutely hated Alabama! Why did my parents move me to such a God forsaken place? How could these kids be so mean and ugly? And why would a parent condone such behavior? I really couldn't understand. This was a defining moment in my life. I really don't believe that Alice was prejudice. I just believe that she succumbed to the pressure of her friends in order to "fit in" with them. I knew then that it didn't matter that the majority of my friends in Miami were White or Hispanic. I was now in a new place, space and evidently a new dispensation in time where this race thing was real, and I had to gird myself up accordingly.

The following year was 8th grade. Things got much better. The entire Tuscaloosa school system had been integrated and now everyone was being bused. That meant that now Black kids on the West side of town were bused to the East side and White kids on the East side were being bused to the West side of town. I was now back in a somewhat diverse learning environment. That really did help my self-esteem and productivity.

Once again, I felt like I fit in. I no longer felt like an outsider because there were other students around that looked like me and that I could identify with.

My years in school become increasingly easier. I tried out for cheerleader in 9th and 10th grade and made the squad both years. I took a break my 11th grade year and then my senior year I tried out for the marching band's dance team. I made the dance team and that was probably the most fun year of my high school life.

I continued to have good grades and excel in advanced classes. Boys were a somewhat non-entity for me. I was attractive, but not really considered a beauty or a "hot babe" so I didn't get a lot of attention. I did get some attention though. Some boys would flirt; every now and then some would call, but nothing serious that I can really remember. Well at least not until my senior year.

Senior year brought about two significant events in my life. First, I "settled" into a relationship with a steady beau! Unknowing to me; this relationship would set precedence for future relationships. The second and most important of the two events was that I became deathly ill during the second semester. Though somewhat vague now, I do recall becoming so ill that I couldn't function. I couldn't do normal things like walk to school, stay awake, complete homework assignments and many days I could not attend school. I had a severe bleeding condition that God literally healed me of. During this time my studies suffered so much that I lost my academic ranking. It was a miracle that I was able to complete my finals and graduate with my class (CHS 1984).

After high school, I attended community college for a year. I tell people that I was too poor to pay for college and too rich to qualify for grants. During this time, I also made the decision that I could no longer live with my parents or grandparents and decided to join the US Armed Forces at 19 years old. Yes, it was that simple. I left life as I knew it, which also included my beau.

CHAPTER 2 - WHY DID I GET MARRIED?

I JOINED the Army in October of 1985. I successfully completed Basic Training (physical combat training) at Fort Jackson in South Carolina. I also trained for my Military Occupation Skill (Clerk Typist – 71L) at Fort Jackson. I completed my AIT as an honor graduate which offered me the opportunity to attend a second AIT for an advanced MOS (Executive Administrative Assistant – 71C) at Fort Benjamin Harrison, Indiana. After graduation, I received orders for III Corps and Fort Hood, Fort Hood, Texas which is located in the small city of Killeen, Texas only 30 minutes away from Austin, Texas.

Between leaving Fort Benjamin Harrison, Indiana and arriving at Fort Hood, Texas I made a stop in my hometown of Tuscaloosa, Alabama for approximately one week. During this week I was reacquainted with a high school classmate that I had a small crush on during my junior year. He had also joined the Army around the same time I did. Less than a week later I left Tuscaloosa, Alabama heading to Fort Hood, Texas pregnant with his child.

So, the thing about the military that I haven't mentioned is that in 1986 when I joined it was a male dominated armed forces. The ratio was somewhere near 300 men per each woman. Needless to say, there wasn't a shortage of men.

When I arrived at Fort Hood, Texas, attention was inevitable. I was a woman in the middle of a barren land, and we were scarce in number. And so, it began. A couple of guys competed for my attention. Now keep in mind that I was pregnant for the first time in life and had no idea that I was. I just thought that I was extremely hot and tired due to the Texas sun and dry heat.

My now ex-husband just happened to be one of the guys vying for my attention. As a matter of fact, he boldly took my attention from a regular suitor within the very first few days on post.

I found him to be fun, comical and caring. There was something genuine about him. I didn't know that meeting him in that moment would be the beginning of a long future with him.

The relationship with him moved quickly. Most military relationships do. Once I told him that I thought I was pregnant I expected things to change. I felt alone, I was scared, and I was not ready to become a mother. I expressed all of this to him. I remember him telling me that the only reason I didn't want to have the baby is because I wanted to continue to be a cover girl! I laugh now when I think about that. That was not the reason I wasn't ready to have a baby. I was not thinking about beauty or my body. I was thinking about my life changing in such a drastic way, without my planning or permission, that I was not prepared for on so many levels.

After my pregnancy was confirmed, I contacted my son's biological father to inform him of the news. First, he questioned the paternity. Then he validated that he knew my character and that he was sure the baby was his. After that, he still asked me if I would consider an abortion. This would be his second child and I would be his second "baby mama". I told him that I didn't want to because it was my first pregnancy (baby). But after he suggested it, I did consider it momentarily. At that moment I felt abandoned. I felt that I didn't have a choice. I never dreamed that I would conceive a baby with a man that wouldn't be interested in fathering his child.

I told my future husband about the conversation. He immediately stopped me from thinking of abortion as an option. He believed that all babies come from God and honestly, so did I. In that very moment, he told me that I could and should have my baby and that he would take care of us. That was it. That was my big marriage proposal. And I accepted it.

We actually did not get married right away. I wanted to wait until after my baby was born to see if he still felt the same way about us. So, a short time after my son turned two months old, we got married.

Why did I get married?

It is impossible to accurately answer the question "why" because it is so subjective. There are numerous reasons why, many I still cannot identify to this date. The simple answer is, I got married because he (my boyfriend) wanted to marry me. That's the truth. Yes, I did love him as much as I knew what love was at the time. Yes, I did enjoy his companionship. I really liked him as a human being and I honestly had an amazing time with him in bed. All of this and he wanted to take care of me and my baby. What other reason did we need to get married? Little did I know that I would soon find out that there were many other reasons and a completely different purpose for marriage.

I thought marriage was going to answer all of my problems and my feelings of inadequacy and rejection. My unrealistic expectations were through the roof.

Keep in mind that I was pregnant by a young man that I really wanted a future with, at the time. When he questioned the baby's paternity, major feelings of rejection and embarrassment filled every part of my mind and body. It was a pain so deep that I could not put it into words.

I was a good girl. I followed all the rules directed by my parents and those in authority. I treated people right; I was polite and well mannered. In addition to all of this, I was not promiscuous, a whore or a thot. I was very selective with who I shared my heart and body with. So why would or could this happen to me? How could any man mistreat or devalue me to that degree?

I quickly realized that my new husband was in no way equipped to handle my feelings of inadequacy and rejection or the results of the trauma that I had experienced in different forms throughout my life. Believe me when I say, I tried to get what I needed out of him, but it was impossible. ***I finally had to realize that people can only give you what that have. You cannot get out of anyone what is not in them.*** While I was depleting him, I did not realize that I had an equal responsibility and obligation to give to him as much as I expected to receive from him.

Marriage has a way of showing you all of your holes from places where you have been damaged and abused. All the issues of rejection, abandonment and your brokenness all come out of hiding after you say your vows.

Yes, life comes for you quickly after the wedding!

Answer the question: Why Did I Get Married?
(Explore your truth about why you got married what your expectations were)

CHAPTER 3 - I'S MARRIED NOW!

THERE IS a reason that *fornication* is called sin in the bible and we are commanded to *flee* from it. Sex seduces you in a way that takes your senses. Your commonsense leaves, your logic vanishes and anything practical seems absurd. Before we got married, I recall a minister asking if I would consider marriage counseling first. I responded "No, I don't really think we need it." What rock was I living under? The rock called "sin" and "fantasy".

The day we got married, we got dressed-up like real adults and drove to the county courthouse, completed an application and waited until we were called. It was me, my new husband and my son sitting in the hall of a Texas courthouse waiting for our number to come up. I don't recall telling anyone what we were planning. The

AFTER THE RIP.

couple that married in the judge's chambers right before us was dressed in all leather motorcycle attire. They were touching, kissing, laughing and smiling. We smiled at them as they walked out and we walked in. As we walked past the threshold, I was fine. I was smiling, I was happy. And then the ceremony began. It was as if all of a sudden I realized that I was really getting married and that I was really giving my life to another human being who had only been on earth as long as I had; actually, less time than I had. I was 21 and he was 20. As the judge started asking us to recite our vows, I began to cry; actually, I began to sob uncontrollably. I cried so hard and with such pain, that the judge stopped the ceremony and had me join him in his private conference room adjacent to his chambers. He asked me if someone was forcing me to marry my fiancé. He asked if my life was in danger and if I was afraid of him. He said that if I wasn't ready and wanted to end the ceremony right then that I could and that he would protect me. I replied "No" to all of the questions. He then said that by law he had to obey my wishes but that in his best judgement I should not be getting married, at least not that day. But I had to do it. I didn't want to embarrass my fiancé or myself. And so, I wiped my tears, took a deep breath, re-entered the judge's chambers and we proceeded with the marriage vows. Now understand, my fiancé was having his own little struggle as well. At one point, while repeating his vows, he said that he took me to be his "awful leaded wife" (true story). But finally it ended. Whew, we did it! We were pronounced husband and wife; we were married! We were married on a Friday. Now, our new lives would start together. And so, it did!

So, I'm married. Now what? Perhaps we should have thought and talked this through a little longer and little more seriously. I now understand that marriage is for the grown and sexy. There is no place for immaturity in this union.

Before we married, things were fun and seemed pretty light. It didn't seem as if there were any problems that I could recall. Of course, I would not have recognized any of the problems anyway because I was so seduced with sex and orgasms that I missed pretty much every red flag that was waving on his side of the room and he definitely missed the flags waving on mine.

I don't recall anyone really being happy for us. Well, no one in our immediate families. His mom was definitely not happy, and my parents were basically going along with my decision. The only issue is that no one could give us a reason why we shouldn't get married or be together. Grant it, there were hundreds of reasons we shouldn't have married. Yet, no one could really articulate it to us in a way that we could comprehend.

Now two young people who didn't know themselves and who definitely didn't know each other had connected their lives and joined together as one. But what exactly were we joining together?

We were joining together all of the unresolved issues of our childhoods that were waiting dormant for this time in space. These unresolved issues included all the fears, disappointments, abuse, neglect, abandonment, heartbreak, mistrust and lack of understanding; and it was all now coupled in one household, under one roof... legally!

If only we could have looked past our physical smiles, his libido and my long legs and were able to see the devastated little boy and the bruised little girl that we were getting ready to meet within the next few months and years, I'm sure we both would have made different decisions.

It didn't take long for the reality of my marriage to manifest in disappointments, life changing decisions, and the pain inflicted by placing unrealistic expectations and unwritten and verbalized contracts on each other.

Honestly, we struggled from day one! Embarrassing but true. There are so many events that took place in the first few years that neither of us ever recovered from.

So, there we were just a few months into our marriage and I was seriously contemplating leaving him. As a matter of fact, I went as far as calling my parents and my grandparents to let them know that I thought I had made a mistake and that I wanted to get out of the marriage. My parents and grandparents gave me the same advice. You've only been married a few months and marriage can be hard. I was told that we were in our adjustment stage and that I needed to stay and work it out. They would not welcome me home, because I was married now!

Now, even though my marriage eventually ended in divorce, I definitely thank God for the stance of my family. They stood for marriage and encouraged me to do the right thing. Had I left my husband then, my second and third sons would never have been born and I am sure that my marriage was ordained of God for that very reason.

And so… after countless life events, three states, two more sons, falling in and out of love with each other, birthdays, birthday parties, children's school plays, parent teacher meetings, church fellowships, graduations, a 10 year Wedding Vow Renewal, date nights, bills, houses, lies, affairs, screams, fights, tears, a miscarriage, an abortion, a few separations and a few reconciliations; finally, 14 years later…my marriage officially ended. In December 2001 we divorced.

I have to admit that at the time my marriage ended, I did not want a divorce. I wanted "us" to work out. I wanted our family to remain intact. I was now the mother of three sons; three Black men in America. I didn't want to be a cliché or stereotype and most of all I didn't want my sons to be a stereotype… the proverbial "fatherless little black boys" raised by a struggling single mother. I had seen enough of that scene on television and portrayed by so many people I knew in real life.

So, honestly, I fought it! I fought it for a while. I fought for the marriage for a year after my husband told me that he wanted a divorce. I had considered divorce many times during the marriage, but I never asked for one. This was shocking to me. Did he really want a divorce? We had only moved to Atlanta from North Carolina a little less than a year from the time he made that announcement to me. I thought the plan was for us to raise our sons in an affluent city where they could see black men "win"! I thought the plan was to raise our sons in a church where they saw solid families. Families where men were leaders and women and children were well taken care of. I thought the plan was for us to retire at 40 and grow old together. This divorce thing was not quite a part of the plan that we had been discussing. I prayed, I begged, I sought counseling, I had anointed people praying for us, for me, for my marriage.

I talked to my Godmothers and asked for advice. After all they were voices of wisdom. They were or had been married and could help me keep this situation under control.

So, the advice I was given was not at all what I expected to hear. Meaning, no one would give me the answer. Everyone kept saying and I kept hearing pray, listen to the Lord and obey.

Well that was it. That's what I had to do because clearly, I was not going to receive any direction other than that from the people that I honored and trusted.

We were now living in Atlanta, GA, attending a popular mega church and living in a beautiful middle-class neighborhood in a 5-bedroom, 3 full bath, 3000 square foot home with a 2-car garage. This was far from our lifestyle in NC. There, we lived in a 3-bedroom, 1 bath, ranch style home with no garage. That house was nice, and it was what we decided to start in so that we could make sure that we could afford to send our children to private Christian school. But in Atlanta, the school system was better, the family support unit was stronger, and our earnings were much larger. We could finally live the *American Dream*... once we figured out what it was.

So, I began to pray! And I prayed, and I prayed, and I prayed. And it seemed that God wasn't hearing me. Or at least it seemed that he wasn't answering my prayers if He heard them.

At that time, I was working as a facilities manager part time at a major consulting firm in Atlanta. I really enjoyed my job because I started working late in the mornings and ended work early in the evenings. I worked 6 hours a day which was ideal for dropping my sons at school and picking them up in the evenings. It also helped me dodge Atlanta rush hour traffic that lasted three hours for both the commute to and from work. My husband basically transferred with his agency from Charlotte, NC to Atlanta, GA.

My position placed me in an atmosphere of millionaires, the very wealthy and elite society. I was exposed to people from all over the world and lifestyles that I had no clue even existed. At that firm, I learned that medical doctors do still make "house calls", as a matter of fact, they make "office calls". Tailors come to your office as well as other professionals. There was even a full-time concierge to take care of time-consuming tasks that the company partners, their spouses, nannies, assistants or housekeepers didn't have time to do. Yes, it was a much different world than I had ever been exposed to.

The IT guy at the firm was a devout Christian. From time to time he and I would pass a warm "praise him" between us. He was also from Africa; I can't remember which country. He had recently gotten engaged and invited me to his wedding. I was excited to attend because he was really a great guy and he told me that it would be a traditional African wedding. I always had a deep love and affection for all things African…and so I was really ready for this experience. I attended his wedding and to my surprise it was an amazing spiritual experience. Oh, let me add that it lasted at least 5 hours which I was definitely not expecting, but I hung in there. The spirit of God was so strong during the ceremony that I decided that I would make plans to visit his church in the Sundays to come.

By this time my marriage was actually becoming pretty unbearable. My husband was spending a lot of time away from home "working" and going to military drills on weekends. I was extremely lonely and was feeling as if I'd lost my best friend. I don't know that I had ever thought of my husband even as a friend, but when he was no longer present in spirit, I realized that there was a time that he really was my friend. I realized that there was a time that the only person I wanted to share the details of my day with was him. I also realized that he was the first person I always thought of to share a funny joke with. Unfortunately, he was also the person that I complained to the most about everything including his shortfalls. And now... I was missing that. I was missing the comfort of his strength, his loyalty, his encouragement, his calm demeanor and his protection. The strange thing about protection is that you don't realize how much you have, until you no longer have it. I was never afraid to stay home alone with the kids or without them. That's because I knew at some point my husband would walk through the door and take care of everything. As soon as he left mentally, emotionally and physically, I felt uneasy about the security of the house. I constantly started checking the doors and on the children throughout the night. In those days I etched the Lord's Prayer in my heart and on my lips. I was starting to depend on the God in ways I hadn't before.

One Sunday morning, a few weeks after attending my colleagues wedding ceremony, I decided that I would attend his church. I prepared the Saturday before, because I had not only had to dress myself but assist 3 young boys and their cousin to make sure they were decently dressed, fed breakfast and off to church on the other side of Atlanta. That early morning, I spent a little time praying; basically, asking God to order my steps, and send me direction concerning my marriage. I heard him clearly this morning "Release Him". I was a bit heartbroken by what I thought was God's voice, but I wasn't really sure. Why would the

God that ordained marriage give me an answer that I thought was so contrary to His word? But I didn't let that slow me down. I was ready to hear the word and be a part of the anointed worship I had experienced at the wedding.

I will never forget this day as long as I live. After driving for 40 minutes on an early Sunday morning in Atlanta, I found the church. It wasn't at all what I expected. It was a small brick church sitting in the middle of the "hood" in Atlanta. At that time, I was a member of an elaborate mega church that seated at least 25,000; so of course, everything else was small to me. We entered the service and just as I had expected, the worship service was anointed and different than what I had been experiencing. There were tongues and tongues of interpretation, prophesying, and intense worship. At one point in the service right after the Pastor finished ministering, he called me up to the front of the church. He said the Lord had directed him to pray for me. He took a bottle of anointing oil (the same bottle that he had poured a dab into his palms to lay hands on many others) and poured the oil from the bottle on top of my head until it was dripping unto my forehead. He said that the Lord sent me there to prepare me for the fiery trial that I was getting ready to walk through. He assured me that I would make it out victoriously. He told me about the prayer that I prayed just that morning before I left for church and that God wanted me to know that He heard me, He answered me and that He would take care of me.

After that word, I stood there crying and praising God, scared, happy, sad and in awe that I could and did hear God's voice!

And so, from that day, I agreed to a divorce. I no longer tried to convince my husband to stay with me or us. I no longer tried to be sweeter and make him happy. I no longer inquired where he was going or where he had been. I did still care; however, I was at complete peace; yet I still had a broken heart! Most of the divorced folks that have ever had a similar journey totally understand this statement and this position.

It took me an entire year to realize that if you beg them to stay, you'll have to continue to beg them not to leave. If you beg them not to leave, you'll have to continue to beg them to stay. In other words, the departure is inevitable… you'll only prolong the time and suffering. **Never beg!**

CHAPTER 4 - THE TRAUMA NAMED DIVORCE!

DIVORCE IS DEEMED a trauma (a wound) because it is just that. As discussed in the introduction to the book, divorce is a violent ripping of the marriage covenant. It is devastating and causes a deep painful wound to the mental, spiritual, emotional and physical body.

So, the man that asked me for the divorce did not want to file for the divorce; I could never get a clear answer from him as to why he didn't want to file. Perhaps somewhere in his logic, if he didn't file, then he wasn't the perpetrator or the villain in the process. Now, although my husband did not want to file, he did try negotiating with me concerning the marital assets and custody of our sons. To say the least, every one of his proposals were preposterous to me. I felt almost forced to secure an attorney and file for the divorce in order to ensure custody of our sons and gain fair equity of our marital assets in the separation.

Now, there are some words I clearly remember saying to my husband because I wanted to make a major impact on his memory of this time period. I stated that "the one thing you will remember about the divorce is that I begged you to pray with me and to consider your sons." As a matter of fact, that was one of the last statements I made before the circus, called court proceedings, started.

The process of ripping your life apart or divorcing can be brutal, abusive, emotional, disruptive, scary, terrorizing and, as I mentioned before, down-right devastating! Unfortunately, in my opinion and from my perspective, the court system of lawyers, judges, mediators and the like seemed to use this extremely vulnerable situation to take advantage of the brokenhearted and distressed.

It appears that everyone is getting paid with your money, except for you (and your children). Attorneys charge an astronomical amount of money for every bit of information they give you and every second of every answer they provide to you, even if they have already provided you with the same information via a phone voicemail message, email message, or a 15 minute conversation they have with you after church in the parking lot right after, "praise the Lord Sis!" Yes, they are all billable minutes. If you have a lot of heartache and pain and are confused about the entire process the more lucrative you are to your attorney. I'm not making this up. I only wished someone had told me this before I hired one.

I felt that my attorney played on my emotions. She interpreted my pain into words that are forever etched on paper and filed as a public document that the entire world has access to. And even though I may have had a lot of the emotions at that particular moment in time, it was just that. It was that moment in time, and that particular moment only lasted a few months. According to my divorce papers, my marriage was a terrible entity that never should have formed and needed to be dissolved as soon as possible. Not true.

To be clear, I am not an advocate for divorce! I am and will forever be an advocate for marriage and family. I am an advocate for forgiveness and reconciliation. Even though my marriage did not survive the attacks against it, I truly believe and know that marriages can thrive even after heartbreak and devastation. With your permission, God can and will breathe life into the deadest of situations. I've seen Him do it!

So, there I was, court date, after court date, tear after tear, sleepless night after sleepless night for almost a year. The divorce process darkened the very existence of my life. Yet I continued to breathe, live, work and care for my children and household through it all. Now, I didn't say that I was great at any of those things; I simply remember being able to perform normal duties as I carried what felt like my heart, dripping blood, around in my hand every day.

I'm sure that many people noticed, but not many

said words to me. I think lots of people cared, I just don't think we've been equipped as a society to deal with such broken people in such volatile and broken situations. So, since they didn't know what to say, most didn't say anything. I'm not sure what my response would have been to anyone that would have asked about the process that I was deeply thrust into. I recall an uncle telling me that my children didn't have me or anyone to assist them in certain areas of life at that time and that was causing them to act out; however, I don't recall him or anyone else offering any assistance in resolving any of those problems. Nor do I remember really understanding, having the capacity, strength or desire to understand what the problems were either. All I could concentrate on was that I had to work in order to buy food to cook and feed to my children. I made sure they had clean clothes, made it to school on time, and completed their homework, as much as possible. I took them to practices almost every day. My three sons were actively involved in T-ball, football and track. Being busy helped me keep a regime that kept my house "floating." I had so much to do, that I didn't have time to think of having an official "nervous breakdown." Now understand, I am quite sure that I had a mini nervous breakdown; however, time did not permit for a full one.

I thought to myself day after day that I couldn't live the way I was living. I couldn't possibly be expected to dedicate my entire life just to be a caregiver and provider. Yet every day, I woke up, got up and I did it again. Pretty soon weeks turned into months and months turned into years.

By the third year of the divorce my emotions started to stabilize. I know, right? It's shocking to hear me admit that I was still heartbroken and devastated three-years into a divorce. Not everyone experiences grief on this level, for this long; however, it's pretty common. As a matter of fact, I've talked to and counseled lots of people (men and women alike) that admitted that their grieving process took much longer than three years.

You can actually fall-in-love and decide to marry someone within months, but it takes years to recover from that quick decision.

A MOMENT OF TRANSPARENCY FOR MARRIED COUPLES

A MOMENT OF TRANSPARENCY FOR MARRIED COUPLES

There are many seasons in marriage. Every relationship has its ups and downs. Most people, like myself, are not divorced because we no longer loved our spouses, even though we may have felt we didn't love them anymore at that time. I am divorced because I did not know how important it was for me to love, support, build up, discern the covenant breaking spirit (Jezabel) and cover my spouse (and family) in continual, war-like prayer. I was so busy trying to change him into what I wanted that I missed the good man that he already was. Now understand, he missed the good woman that I was as well. The answer is not to complain, fuss, argue or make your point. Both parties sooner or later grow weary physically, emotionally, mentally and spiritually in those stressful situations. As a woman I worked just as hard as my husband and made as much money as he did; took care of our three sons, the house and other obligations and responsibilities. So why shouldn't I have equal "say and authority" in the family? Why? Because, the Bible said I didn't...that's why (Ephesians 5:22-23). So while I was unconsciously consumed by how tired and unfulfilled I was, the covenant breaking spirit did her job! What I've learned from Divorce is...

(1) It would have been easier to take my God ordained position as a wife than be the head of a 1-head household with the same amount of responsibility and less resources.

(2) My money only added to the quality of my beautiful lifestyle; it could not and did not fund my lifestyle. When his money left, I felt it!

(3) TIP, TIP, TIP... If your household duties are overwhelming, then pay for domestic help. Having someone clean, wash and cook a few times a week will save your life (time, stress, energy) and your family!

(4) You can accomplish more in prayer than you can with physical words. Communication is important, but reconciliation is more important (as my Apostle Travis Jennings often says, it doesn't matter who's right; the most important thing is to reconcile).

(5) Child Support is a fraction of a fraction of a fraction of what a household requires to adequately take care of children even when both parties have high incomes. (Yes, I paid child support too).

Yes, I can and will marry again...with a different perspective and of course being a much different person in a much different place in life. However, real talk, it will never be with the same family dynamic. Divorce destroys, changes and affects every person in that family in some way. I saw it in my children, myself, my ex-spouse and our extended families and friends.

By the way, my ex-husband and I are extremely cool and have a great relationship now.

Divorce isn't usually the answer, though it seems so in a weary season. Reconsider that option; seek counseling, talk to your spiritual leaders and make a decision to allow God to save what He has ordained.

Through the years that I have spent counseling survivors of divorce, I've heard a common statement by most, **"I wouldn't wish this process or pain on my worst enemy."** The entire process of divorcing is so traumatic that most people don't see it as being worth all of the pain and suffering, length of time and all the money it all costs.

It is so important to invest in your marriage via strong couples ministries, counseling, vacations, time together, etc. Unfortunately, my marriage started out in survival mode when it really should have started in the divorce prevention mode.

DISCLAIMER: Everyone has a different path, story, circumstance or situation in marriage. I am not encouraging anyone to stay in abusive relationships. I am speaking from my experience in a normal average marriage and family. Seek counsel.

CHAPTER 5 - THE GRIEVING PROCESS!

ACCORDING to experts and from my knowledge and experience, divorce rarely comes without some degree of pain and grief. Most people do not get married with the intention of divorcing. Unfortunately, many marriages today do not survive, and the resulting heartache can be overwhelming. Like any loss, the end of a marriage will usually trigger a variety of emotions and reactions. It doesn't matter if you were the spouse that wanted to keep the marriage or that filed for the divorce, you will still experience some level of pain. Yes, even if you are the person that wants out of the marriage, you may be surprised that ending the marriage will still invoke grief.

Many people experience five to seven distinct stages of grief, including **shock, denial, anger, bargaining,**

depression, testing and **acceptance.** I definitely experienced 6 of the 7 stages. Some stages I experienced more than once.

1. SHOCK

This is an emotional paralysis on receiving the bad news! I was definitely shocked by the announcement that my ex-husband wanted a divorce. The first time he said it, honestly, I ignored it. However, once he repeated it, I knew that he was serious. I could not imagine that he really wanted a permanent out. After all that we had been through to build our lives to the point where we were finally thriving, I could not have imagined that I would ever hear those words. At first, I could not move, I could not respond, my heart was beating so fast. Each breath became deeper and my throat started to get dry. He seemed to say it without any remorse, any emotion or any sympathy for my feelings or disposition. I walked around for days in disbelief. I even questioned whether or not I had dreamed the entire conversation with him; but, once he entered the house after his workday with no warmth and without giving me any attention, I knew that the conversation had been real.

2. DENIAL

When a marriage comes to an end, the loss can be terribly surprising and difficult to digest. You may have trouble believing and accepting that the relationship is over. Denial is explained as a type of defense mechanism that softens the immediate shock and protects us from the pain of loss.

To protect my mind and my emotions, I told myself that my husband was going through a mid-life crisis. The only problem was that he was only 33 years old at the time. I also decided that he was only talking crazy because he had recently lost his father and he was still grieving, processing and recovering from that loss. Some of this may have actually been a factor; however, regardless of the events that may have triggered his decision; I was in true denial of his decision. I decided that I would just "wait it out". After all, he was obviously not in his right frame of thinking, therefore; I would exercise a little love and patience until he realized that he was being foolish. Day in and day out, nothing got better. He continued to enter the house after his workday with no warmth and without giving me any attention. We did not resume conversations, touching, kissing, hugging or sex. The one characteristic of my husband was that he was extremely sexual with me. Once he became distant in this regard, I knew that the marriage was in deep trouble. I could not continue to pretend that the relationship would be magically restored. I tried to convince him to participate in counseling and listen to more seasoned couples to help us get through this rough season that we were going through. None of this really worked. He did participate in a counseling session or two, but he was never really present or in the moment for them. Once a person has made a real decision, there is usually no convincing them to change their minds. It was clear that he had checked out.

3. ANGER

Once reality has sunk in, many people experiencing divorce become angry. You may feel resentful of your partner for things he did or said, or you may be upset with yourself for your own actions that contributed to the end of the marriage. During this stage of grief, emotions can become increasingly intense. A person often concentrates on the things he hates about his partner, his own regrets or the things he feels guilty about. It is a time of blame, irritation and disgust. Displaced anger is common, and you may find yourself having less patience and becoming easily aggravated with day-to-day tasks or situations.

Angry, mad, pissed... are just a few words to describe how I started feeling. The shock quickly grew into anger. I looked up and thought to myself "how dare this joker think that he has the right to leave me?" After all the crap I subjected myself to over the course of the 14 years I had been with him, he had the nerve to think it was okay to quit! If I didn't quit, he didn't have the right to quit. How dare he leave me with 3 young sons to raise alone. How dare we build our dream house together, start a new chapter in life and throw it all away because of his early mid-life crisis! I was mad about everything! Waking up, getting up, preparing breakfast, managing my sons, dressing myself and even combing my hair became exhausting. At many points throughout the day I would think about the actual marriage ceremony and how I was given an "out" that I refused to take, because I didn't want to embarrass my husband or myself. If I had taken it, then I wouldn't be suffering this loss now. I would never have had to know this pain, this rejection, this betrayal. I thought about it so much until I almost ran myself crazy. I would start sweating, crying and would become dizzy with anxiety.

4. BARGAINING

Bargaining is a last-ditch attempt at coming to terms with the decision to divorce. It is described as a time when you try to repair the damaged marriage or convince yourself that divorce is the right decision. This stage is often prompted by panic, fear and the desire to regain control. You may try to negotiate with your partner in an effort to correct what went wrong, or you may remind yourself of the reasons the relationship did not work.

I was hurt, confused, angry and heartbroken, yet something in me still wanted my marriage and most of all I wanted my family to stay intact. My husband and I had been through many seasons in the marriage, so this was just another season to me. So once again, I mustered up the strength and energy to try to convince him that divorcing was not the best option for us or our sons. The more I talked and pleaded, the more bored he become with my words and attempt to reason with him. Embarrassed by my failed attempts to convince my husband to change his mind, I started thinking about all the things that I could remember that he had ever said or done to hurt me. I grasped for anything that would give me a reason to convince myself that the marriage was never a good one. During this time, I tried to convince myself that divorcing would not be the big loss that I was making it out to be. It was all in my mind and I would be fine.

5. DEPRESSION

Depression is a condition of general emotional dejection and withdrawal; sadness greater and more prolonged than that warranted by any objective reason. It usually sets in as a person understands that the marriage is truly over. Many upsetting decisions and adjustments take place in the aftermath of a divorce, which can lead to deep sadness. Depression is often accompanied by shame, and many people experience a period of isolation while grieving.

For me, sleeping was usually easy because I was so exhausted from all of the activities of the day that I collapsed from exhaustion most nights. However, some nights I would awaken to a severe chest pain which was my heart hurting so badly that I could feel my physical body ache. Initially, the grieving felt as if someone had died. Actually, when I think about it, it felt as if I had died without being buried. I was still walking around the earth as the "living dead." The heartache and pain was unbearable some days. Mornings were the worse. I would wake up with such a spirit of heaviness sitting on my chest that it felt like a human being was crushing my lungs with their full body weight. I lost a lot of weight, which was the reason I was exhausted. I didn't have an appetite and was not eating enough food to create enough energy for the amount of daily activities that I participated in. I was underweight, tired, depressed and slowly dying on the inside with my physical body catching up. My husband was spending more time away from the house and I was growing extremely lonely, tired and was mentally exhausted. I had so much embarrassment and shame. My husband and I were the spiritual family of my siblings. We were the family that gave all the advice on family, relations and finances. How was it possible for us to be failing all areas after being the family subject matter experts? At one point my brothers offered to talk to my husband. I asked them not to and they respected my wishes. My brothers were protective, and I didn't want to see our issues turn into a family feud. Anyway, I knew that my husband's mind was made-up, and he wasn't going to listen to them. If his mother, brothers, favorite cousins and preachers hadn't reached him, surely my brothers' efforts would have been a mute effort as well. I finally realized that I had done all that I could do. I had nothing left. The marriage was really over.

Tip for a Peaceful Night's Sleep: In order to sleep

peacefully during the night, I started playing recordings of messages from church services and praise and worship music throughout the night. I usually fell asleep before the end of the messages. I set a timer so that praise and worship music would start playing an hour before my alarm clock would sound in the morning. This was an effective way for me to combat the spirit of depression that was ready to greet me early in the mornings. I discovered that this was not such a new discovery; it was already available for me to apply according to scripture:

I Samuel 16:23 ~ "Whenever the evil spirit from God bothered Saul, David would play his harp. Saul would relax and feel better, and the evil spirit would go away."

"Jesus called his twelve disciples to him and gave them authority to drive out impure spirits and to heal every disease and sickness...Heal the sick, raise the dead, clean se those who have leprosy, drive out demons. Freely you have received; freely give." ~ Matthew 10:1-8

6. TESTING

In this stage you are trying to seek out realistic solutions to the bad news. Here is where true recovery begins. You start checking to see if you can handle situations you have avoided before. You experiment with laughter and enjoying yourself. You might even test the possibility of loving connections with others at this point, if you've been avoiding that. This is a very important part of the stages of grief, because it is the first movement out of the darker emotions and into the brighter aspects of life.

In this stage I started to remember that I enjoyed outings and activities. I had been so concentrated on the divorce and the negative aspects of the relationship that I lost sight of anything else... like living. I started hanging out at movies and specifically ensured that I only watched comedies. It helped me start to laugh again, which really helped decrease my stress.

7. ACCEPTANCE

In the last stage of grief, you finally come to accept the divorce as part of your life. You embrace the guidance and support of others and slowly begin to let go of negative emotions. The heartache may not be gone, but you are able to resume your normal activities without overwhelming sadness.

Finally, I accepted the truth. My marriage was over. I'm not sure when it actually happened, but it did. Day after day for months, I had to speak out loud, "Kimberly, it is what it is. This marriage is ending, but you are just beginning." Now, as I was speaking this out loud every day, I admit that I did not believe a word of it. As an act of my will I was speaking life. I made a conscious decision to be intentional about shaping my future. After all, I was a Christian and I knew that this was a test of my faith. If I cracked under the pressure, I would be demonstrating my lack of faith in God. During those moments I held on to the scripture that God would not allow more than I could bare (1 Cor 10:13). Since I was experiencing this divorce, then surely, I could bare it.

Acceptance is the last of the stages of grief; however, no stage has a designated length of time that you experience any of the emotions or turmoil that go with the process. You process through each particular stage as long as you need to process. On occasion, you can also return to one of the stages of grief. After I accepted that the divorce was inevitable, I returned to the stage of anger. I actually went through this stage a time or two over the course of a few years. No, not a few weeks or months... a few years.

CHAPTER 6 - MAKING THE DECISION TO FORGIVE

THE FIVE TO SEVEN stages of grief during the divorce process dispel the myth or belief that most people can or should "just get over it!" You learn to accept and deal with the reality of your situation, but please know that making it to the acceptance stage does not usually mean that your pain or heartache will instantly end and you will experience immediate happiness. As a matter of fact, it really is just the beginning of your new normal.

First, know that healing and deliverance is a process.

You must start any new process first by deciding to go through it or to do it.

I decided that I would be divorcing and that I would maintain a sense dignity and respect. In order to do this, I knew that I would have to depend totally on God. I didn't have the answers or the strength to figure out how.

Renewing your mind – do it differently from the world. I'm not sure about others, but I've always heard that the best way to get over someone or heal from a relationship was to get into another relationship as soon as possible. Praise God that I had enough wisdom to realize that was not the route I should take. As a matter of fact, I was sure that part of the issue with most relationships was that no one was taking the time and steps to heal before hooking up with another person. This explains how some people can have multiple marriages and multiple divorces.

Romans 12:2 (NIV) ~ Do not conform to the pattern of this world, but be transformed by the renewing of your mind. Then you will be able to test and approve what God's will is—his good, pleasing and perfect will.

So, there I was, a 34 year-young, beautiful, physically fit, newly single woman after being in a marriage for 14 years.

I believe that one of the best decisions I made was to give myself time to heal before seriously dating again. What I thought was enough time to heal was approximately two years. I should be good, healed and ready to experience real love again after that, right? The only problem was that after two years I was still heartbroken. Even when opportunities presented themselves to me, I was too fearful to actually move into a healthy place or relationship with another man. I had trust issues and was deathly afraid of being hurt or taken advantage of. I couldn't figure out how to move forward. I only knew how to survive to see, live and breathe through another day.

Praise God for prayer, and prayer-warriors. I have to make sure that I add that I was not on this journey alone. No; God had me covered in a blanket of prayer from many different warriors. I had a godmother praying for me without ceasing and speaking the word of the Lord over me, my children and my mind, almost daily. I also had praying grandparents, parents and girlfriends. Do not underestimate the power of prayer or love. God loved me and loves you so much that He ensures that people and angels are in place to cover us in our darkest hours.

Have you ever felt sad, defeated and depressed and all of a sudden, a wind blows through your spirit, leaving you feeling better, out of nowhere? I believe that is when prayer encamps around you to cover, protect and give you peace and strength to continue on your journey.

HOW DO I BEGIN TO HEAL FROM THE PAIN OF DIVORCE?

One word…**Forgiveness;** you have to make a decision to **FORGIVE**. By definition forgive means to excuse for a fault or an offense; pardon; to renounce anger or resentment against. Forgiveness is a choice. You are choosing to offer compassion and empathy to the person who wronged you.

Luke 6:37 (NIV) ~ "Do not judge, and you will not be judged. Do not condemn, and you will not be condemned. **Forgive**, and you will be **forgiven**."

Forgiveness is a gift, not a reward, which means that the person you need to forgive may not be deserving of the gift, just as we are not deserving of God's grace and mercy. It takes faith and humility to forgive.

I am convinced that forgiveness is one of the most important decisions and acts one can ever choose to make.

Unforgiveness will lead to bitterness and a lifetime of resentment. Bitterness defiles everything and everyone around you including you and your mental, physical and spiritual health and well-being.

Matthew 5:44 tells us to "love our enemies and pray for those who persecute you." You must forgive in order to <u>free</u> yourself. Take your eyes and focus off of the perpetrator. Do not allow their actions to be an issue any longer. You now must focus on you (and your children) and your future.

You may be thinking, "how can I or do I forgive"? I've tried, but I still have hurt and feelings of anger."

I learned to forgive by putting my life into perspective. Know that no one can take anything from you or do anything to you that God does not know about.

At first, I prayed to forgive as an act of my will. I would literally pray, "Lord as an act of my will I forgive my ex-husband." The feelings of hurt and pain did not go away immediately. Honestly, I was praying this same prayer and making the confession for at least six months before I realized that I wasn't feeling the same degree of hurt and pain as when I first started praying and confessing. At that point, I no longer had to pray "as an act of my will." I then started to confess, "Lord, I forgive my ex-husband." It became easier and easier every time I made the confession. Praying for my ex-husband softened my heart towards him. The feelings of anger started to subside and after a few years, that anger actually turned into compassion. One important element in the process of forgiving is learning how to manage your expectations.

Managing your expectations is simply that. Just because you have a revelation about forgiving, does not mean that your ex-spouse does too. You may think that since your heart is softening or changing towards them, that they are also changing towards you. You may find yourself met with the same resistance, rudeness and attitude from them that you experienced prior to your decision to forgive them. Don't let this stop you from forgiving them and showing them respect and kindness. Stay focused. Remember that you are not forgiving them for a reaction or change of heart from them. You are forgiving as an act of obedience to God and to free yourself from the bondage and chains that the spirit of unforgiveness will bind you with.

In the Bible, in the book of Genesis starting in the 37th chapter, we read the story of Joseph. Joseph was the youngest of 12 children and the son of his father's old age and of the wife he loved. Joseph's brothers were jealous of him because of his father's love and favor for him. As an act of resentment Joseph was betrayed by his brothers and tricked into a pit where he could not free himself. Guilt would not allow his brothers to leave him there, so they decided to sell him into slavery. He went from the **p**it, to **P**otiphar's House (as a slave), to **p**rison and ultimately to the **p**alace. During the time of this 17-year process, Joseph's father experienced much heartache; Joseph endured unfair treatment and conditions. This pain and process was working for a far more exceeding purpose in the earth. After the process, peace, healing and prosperity came not only for Joseph, but for his family and an entire nation.

Gen 45:5 ~ Now therefore; be not grieved, nor angry with yourselves, that ye sold me hither: for God did send me before you to preserve life.

Gen 45:8 ~ So now it was not you that sent me hither, but God.

Again, know that no one can do anything to you that God does not know about or allow. Just like Joseph's journey, God is allowing this process to produce an amazing outcome in your life and the in lives of others that you are assigned to mentor, guide and assist in healing and deliverance.

According to an article on Forgiveness by Johns Hopkins Medicine publication, unforgiveness and chronic anger puts you into a fight-or-flight mode, which results in numerous changes in heart rate, blood pressure and immune response. Those changes, then, increase the risk of depression, heart disease and diabetes, among other conditions. Forgiveness, however, calms stress levels, leading to improved health.

Our emotions affect our bodies and can cause many physical health problems. Researchers have taken note of the connection between failure and bitterness. According to psychologist Dr. Carsten Wrosch, *"Persistent bitterness may result in global feelings of anger and hostility that, when strong enough, could affect a person's physical health. When harbored for a long-time, bitterness may forecast patterns of biological dysregulation (a physiological impairment that can affect metabolism, immune response or organ function) and physical disease.*

Bitterness can stem from a wide range of events in a person's life. Yes, it can come from unforgiveness of a failed marriage.

Studies have found that the act of forgiveness can reap huge rewards for your health, lowering the risk of heart attack; improving cholesterol levels and sleep; and reducing pain, blood pressure, levels of anxiety, depression and stress. And research points to an increase in the forgiveness-health connection as you age.

Remember that forgiveness is a choice; it is not a feeling.

I believe that when you choose to forgive, you are choosing to release <u>them</u> in order to save <u>you</u>!

CO-PARENTING

You may be thinking that this is a strange place to add the topic of co-parenting. Actually, the subject of co-parenting could and should be a separate book of its own. I intentionally added this topic under the chapter on *Making the Decision to Forgive* because I believe that the only way you can successfully co-parent is to first forgive your ex-spouse.

The reality of most divorces is that there are often little humans attached to two people who have now disengaged. Those little humans unintentionally become **collateral damage (injury inflicted on something other than an intended target)** in this process. The goal in a divorce is never to hurt the people you both love the most, your children. Unfortunately, by sheer placement, it is inevitable that children will be involved in the breakup to a deeper degree than they should.

It is important to do all, that you can to protect your children. They did not ask to be born into your tragedy.

Remember that everyone attached to you and your ex-spouse is affected and infected by the divorce process. Children may show signs of trauma, pain and anxiety over the uncertainty of the atmosphere by acting out. My three sons all reacted differently and portrayed different signs and characteristics from the effects of the trauma and stress.

My eldest son was extremely rebellious and had

bouts of crying in class during school most of the day for weeks at a time. At the time he was in the seventh grade. He became very promiscuous at an early age and started skipping school. He completely lost focus and did not graduate from high school. He did later go on to finish his GED, attended college and became a firefighter for a few years until moving on to another career path.

My middle son was in the 4th grade. He retreated to books, performed magic tricks and placed all of his attention onto his schoolwork and learning. He made extremely good grades and attended a magnet school program around the time of the divorce. Some of this was good, except that he became severely introverted and had a hard time dealing with people. Computers quickly became his best friend until he finished high school.

My youngest son seemed to be the least affected basically because he was so young. He was around 5 years old. However, even though we didn't see drastic signs, there were still clear signs. He developed an extremely hot temper at an early age but managed to learn and apply self-discipline and control over the years. He definitely understood that his life had been disrupted. Suddenly, he was leaving his house to go to another house to visit his dad. He constantly asked when daddy was coming home and kept telling me that he wanted everyone to be friends again.

Every time my sons visited their dad, they would return home discombobulated. It would take an entire day to calm them down. I would fill the bathtub in my bedroom to capacity and allow my youngest son to swim until he wore himself out.

I'm sure that the trauma of leaving their father's presence for another few days or weeks caused this emotional turmoil. It was an extremely emotional time for us all. I assured them that he missed them just as much and couldn't wait to see them again as well. In our case, this was the absolute truth.

Let's pause here for a minute. Parents... DO NOT talk negatively about your children's other parent within the ear gates of your children. I will even add that you should not talk negatively about your children's other parent at all. After all, our words are powerful. If we continue to speak badly, we will notice things getting worse. If we speak positive words of affirmation concerning the parent, those words will form and cause a positive change. The negative words that your children hear about their parent hurt and sting them. You have to remember that they are a product of both parents and see whatever characteristics you are magnifying concerning their parent within themselves, whether positive or negative. This is a potential door for the spirit-of-rejection to enter your children. Don't open the door and if you have...CLOSE IT! When you speak negatively about your ex-spouse, it is more of a reflection on you then it is on them. Why? Because you chose them. If you were so good and all together lovely, how did you make such a terrible choice in a spouse? Exactly. Now, shut-up!

I know that some ex-spouse's make it hard to find anything good to say about them. As most of our parents and grandmother's would say, "If you can't say anything good about a person, then don't say anything." If ever this wisdom holds true, it's in this situation. Your discretion here can save your children's futures and lives.

The reason I know how much a negative impact this tactic has on children is because I was guilty of it in the early stages of the divorce and I see the negative results manifested in my sons even until this day.

I used the same strategy for my sons that I did for myself. They were so active in sports and other school activities that bedtime was never a problem for them. They slept well during the night; however, the spirit of depression would attack them in the mornings the same way it tried to attack me.

Fortunately, I had an intercom system that allowed music to play through speakers in every room of the house. I would start playing praise and worship music before they woke up every morning. Yes, just as it did for me, it also worked for them.

Of course, the most important strategy for my sons was prayer. Not only did I pray for them, I allowed each one of them to pray and read the bible out loud with me as a family as well.

I will not lie and say that my sons are doing great.

Honestly, it's 20 years later and I still see areas where they have yet to recover from this infraction. I kept hearing that children were resilient and that they would be okay before I was. This was not true for my children and the countless other children that are still traumatized by their parent's divorce. Clearly, the people that made those statements did not study the children of divorce.

I will say however, that my sons are blessed, productive and are doing well. They didn't follow the blueprint I wanted them to, but they are responsible adults making their own choices and leading their own lives. They all continue to strive despite some of the issues they are still working through. My ex-spouse and I must live with the consequences of those issues because of our decisions.

I do see God moving in their lives in different capacities and I continue to pray and encourage them to look toward the hills. But most of all, I continue to encourage them to practice forgiveness in their everyday lives.

I am convinced that forgiveness is the key to obtaining your inheritance and seeing the manifestation of promises and prophecies over your life.

~Scriptures on Forgiving~

- Judge not, and you will not be judged; condemn not, and you will not be condemned; forgive, and you will be forgiven. ~Luke 6:37
- Then Peter came up and said to him, "Lord, how often will my brother sin against me, and I forgive him? As many as seven times?" Jesus said to him, "I do not say to you seven times, but seventy times seven. ~Matthew 18:21-22
- And whenever you stand praying, forgive, if you have anything against anyone, so that your Father also who is in heaven may forgive you your trespasses. ~Mark 11:25
- But I say to you who hear, Love your enemies, do good to those who hate you. ~Luke 6:27
- So watch yourselves. "If your brother or sister sins against you, rebuke them; and if they repent, forgive them." ~Luke 17:3

~Scriptures on Healing~

- "He heals the brokenhearted and binds up their wounds." ~Psalms 147:3
- "My son, pay attention to what I say; turn your ear to my words. Do not let them out of

your sight, keep them within your heart; for they are life to those who find them and health to one's whole body." ~ Proverbs 4:20-22
- "A cheerful heart is good medicine, but a crushed spirit dries up the bones." ~ Proverbs 17:22
- "Therefore, confess your sins to each other and pray for each other so that you may be healed. The prayer of a righteous person is powerful and effective." ~ James 5:16
- "He himself bore our sins in his body on the cross, so that we might die to sins and live for righteousness; by his wounds you have been healed." ~ 1 Peter 2:24
- "Peace I leave with you; my peace I give you. I do not give to you as the world gives. Do not let your hearts be troubled and do not be afraid." ~ John 14:27
- "Come to me, all you who are weary and burdened, and I will give you rest. Take my yoke upon you and learn from me, for I am gentle and humble in heart, and you will find rest for your souls. For my yoke is easy and my burden is light." ~ Matthew 11:28-30
- "He gives strength to the weary and increases the power of the weak." ~ Isaiah 40:29
- "No temptation has overtaken you except what is common to mankind. And God is faithful; he will not let you be tempted

beyond what you can bear. But when you are tempted, he will also provide a way out so that you can endure it." ~ 1 Corinthians 10:13

- "Then they cried to the LORD in their trouble, and he saved them from their distress. He sent out his word and healed them; he rescued them from the grave." ~ Psalms 107:19-20
- "LORD my God, I called to you for help, and you healed me." ~ Psalms 30:2
- "The righteous cry out, and the LORD hears them; he delivers them from all their troubles. The LORD is close to the brokenhearted and saves those who are crushed in spirit. The righteous person may have many troubles, but the LORD delivers him from them all; he protects all his bones, not one of them will be broken. Evil will slay the wicked; the foes of the righteous will be condemned. The LORD will rescue his servants; no one who takes refuge (trusts) in him will be condemned." ~ Psalms 34:17-22
- "Praise the LORD, my soul, and forget not all his benefits - who forgives all your sins and heals all your diseases, who redeems your life from the pit and crowns you with love and compassion." ~ Psalms 103:2-4
- "Have mercy on me, LORD, for I am faint; heal me, LORD, for my bones are in agony." ~ Psalms 6:2

- "The LORD protects and preserves them—they are counted among the blessed in the land - he does not give them over to the desire of their foes. The LORD sustains them on their sickbed and restores them from their bed of illness." ~ Psalms 41:2-3
- "The LORD is my shepherd, I lack nothing. He makes me lie down in green pastures, he leads me beside quiet waters, he refreshes my soul. He guides me along the right paths for his name's sake. Even though I walk through the darkest valley, I will fear no evil, for you are with me; your rod and your staff, they comfort me. You prepare a table before me in the presence of my enemies. You anoint my head with oil; my cup overflows. Surely your goodness and love will follow me all the days of my life, and I will dwell in the house of the LORD forever." ~ Psalms 23
- "Hear, LORD, and be merciful to me; LORD, be my help. You turned my wailing into dancing; you removed my sackcloth and clothed me with joy." ~ Psalms 30:10-11
- "My flesh and my heart may fail, but God is the strength of my heart and my portion forever." ~ Psalms 73:26

CHAPTER 7 - JOURNALING

It was during my grieving process that I started to journal. Journaling is an amazing tool that can assist you in keeping your sanity in the process. Some of my journal entries made absolutely no sense to anyone except me. I wrote in code, cursive and many other formats. Sometimes I drew pictures and didn't use words at all. Perhaps, I did this so that if my children stumbled upon the journals, they wouldn't be able to figure out what I was writing about. It was a way of protecting them. Later, I realized that it was also a way to use my bottled up creativity.

I wrote everything. The hardest thing I ever had to do in my journaling was to tell or write the truth. I wrote my most intimate feelings and emotions about my entire life including my divorce process. I also wrote about the part I played in the demise of my relationship, which helped me take ownership of my faults and shortcomings. I was already messed up before I met my ex-husband, or I probably wouldn't have chosen him. And the same for him. Journaling opened a level of healing and deliverance that I had never experienced. In my own private space with my journal and my God I was able to cry, release, pray and see myself and my situation in a brand-new light.

As I journaled, the Lord would speak to me. I heard him clearly tell me, "Do not project any pre-existing issues as faults of your ex-spouse." Pain speaks so loudly! It wants to find someone to blame. In that moment, I could not blame anyone. God took that crutch away.

What exactly does this mean? Well, for example, if you were molested, abandoned, rejected, used and/or abused as a child or young adult, your ex-spouse had nothing to do with that. When you re-visit and re-read your journal entries and notes, look for areas where these infractions took place. In other words, make a conscious effort to find places in your writings where you projected and misdirected your pain that was no fault of your ex-spouse onto him/her. You will be amazed at how much you will discover.

Journaling is also where I discovered my most intimate and anointed times of prayer. I would write detailed prayers, songs of worship and praise. Before I could finish, I would be laid in the floor thanking, praising and worshipping God for His goodness and

His mercy. It was those times that God was holding me, healing me and loving me into a place of unspeakable peace.

Journaling Tip:

Journaling can be extremely emotional and spiritually cleansing. Make sure you have a quiet private space for at least an hour. Be prepared with drinking water and tissue or towels. Make sure that you are physically comfortable. In addition to tears flowing, you may find yourself coughing, getting sick on your stomach, having a sudden urge to use the restroom, vomiting, screaming, crying out from a deep place, etc. Don't be alarmed. This is where your healing and deliverance is beginning. These are signs that unforgiveness and bitterness are being uprooted from the depths of your spirit, soul and psyche.

Understand that God does not waste any pain. Just know that you are in process! No, it does not feel good, but God is working behind the scenes. He is using this process to mature you.

To this day when I am frustrated and in need of therapy, I grab a journal and a pen and start writing.

Journaling Exercise: Who Do I Need to Forgive?
(Yourself, Friends, Family, Church, God)

CHAPTER 8 - DENOUNCING THE SPIRIT OF REJECTION

REJECTION – is a spirit. It must be cast out and denounced! Rejection is defined as the action of rejecting: the state of being rejected. The original meaning of the word rejection was to throw back. Rejection occurs when a person or group of people excludes an individual and refuses to acknowledge or accept them. Abandonment is a similar term, meaning to desert someone, to leave and never return. Rejection usually enters as a result of a trauma (wound).

According to the article "10 Fruits of a Spirit of Rejection At Work In Your Life" offered by Christian Deliverance Ministry here are some signs of rejection and self-rejection:

Signs that you are being tormented by a Spirit of Rejection:

- You find yourself comparing your circumstances or situations with others, and you never seem to measure up.
- You feel like you missed out on life's opportunities and now it's too late.
- No amount of encouragement is enough to convince you of your worth.
- You feel rejected if you are not greeted or acknowledged by leadership.
- You constantly seek the approval of others and suffer from people pleasing.
- You are easily offended or embarrassed from discipline or correction.
- You are always trying to prove yourself in public.
- You feel like you are on the outside looking in during interactions with people.
- You think you could do a better job than the current leader or teacher if you are given the opportunity.
- You believe no one understands you, or what you are going through.

Self-Rejection is a form of bondage that causes you to project feelings and thoughts on others that they didn't feel at all. The same thing happens when you judge yourself, which is also a form of self-rejection.

Signs of Self Rejection:

- Inability to trust God
- Excessive shyness
- Difficulty in loving others
- Self-criticism
- Wishful comparison with others
- Over-attention on clothes
- Floating bitterness
- Perfectionism
- Attitudes of superiority
- Awkward attempts to hide unchangeable defects
- Extravagance
- Wrong priorities

Some people associate their feelings of rejection as being a part of their personality, not realizing that rejection is the controlling or root spirit for those feelings/emotions.

Our personalities are multifaceted. It consists of many different parts. To keep it simple I will divide us into two personality types/and four temperaments:

An introvert – is a shy, reticent person.

An extrovert – is an outgoing, overtly expressive person.

The four temperaments is a proto-psychological theory that suggests that there are four fundamental personality types, **sanguine** (enthusiastic, active, and social), **choleric** (short-tempered, fast, or irritable), melancholic (**analytical, wise**, and quiet), and **phlegmatic** (relaxed and **peaceful**).

I believe that the enemy (the devil) uses our natural temperaments to cover or hide the spirit of rejection.

The spirit of rejection can enter as early as conception. This is direct proof that you were born a threat to the enemy if he had to attack you prior to your birth into the earth realm. Unknowingly, a mother can open a portal to her unborn child. The pregnancy may have been conceived out of wedlock, not planned or unwanted. The spirit of rejection, emotions of torment, and the mother's pain entered into the unborn baby. The child then spends most of his life with feelings of inadequacy, of not being loved, wanted or accepted.

The spirit of rejection also enters in through other formable stages of our lives sub-consciously, although we may be aware of and have memories of events. For instance, the enemy may have you believing that you just are…. who you are. But who are you really?

If you have an <u>introverted</u> personality type and <u>melancholic</u> temperament you may assume that you were born to be very quiet and analytical. You think all the time. You think when you wake up, you think all day, you think on your way to bed and you think during the night when you awake from your sleep. You just naturally don't like to be around a lot of people, noise, movement or adventure. You don't consider yourself fearful; instead you consider your actions and decisions to be careful and wisely thought out, anticipated and planned. You do not take risks. Let me say that again……You DO NOT take RISKS!

Yes, indeed some of the characteristics we display are authentic characteristics of our personalities; however, I believe that a great part of our personality characteristics are our responses to being rejected at an early age.

If during your formative/adolescent years you were constantly told to "be quiet" and sent the message (whether verbal or subliminal) that you were to be seen and not heard or that your thoughts or opinion were not important, you have subconsciously conformed to this message. This is probably the reason you do not have a voice or find it hard to voice your feelings, thoughts of opinions. It's the reason you don't ever have anything to say.

If you were constantly bombarded with expressions that convinced you that you were not capable of performing a task or succeeding or accomplishing a mission, then you more than likely have developed an inferiority complex.

If you audibly heard or if it was implied that people would judge you, not like you, or not accept you for any reason then you are probably a person who suffers greatly from self-rejection. In other words, you never give people a chance to know you, like you or choose you. You already decide for them how they see you, perceive you and feel about you.

How about this one…. You cannot trust anyone! You cannot trust anyone because your entire life you were told verbally and through actions that, "you cannot trust anyone!" All of these messages definitely influenced the way you perceive all people. As time progressed, you started to shy away from crowds of people and personal relationships to protect yourself from being victimized by this world of untrustworthy human beings.

These are classic examples of the enemy using what we think are our natural temperaments to hide this spirit-of-rejection. You are not really shy or quiet; you are afraid! You are afraid because of every message you've ever received. People do like you; you just don't know or accept it because you walk in self-rejection.

You can accomplish anything you put your mind to. You just don't believe it because every idea and task you've ever attempted has been criticized to the point that you gave up trying or failed to complete or accomplish it.

You have spent your entire life running from the PAIN caused by this disrespectful demon and spirit-of-rejection!

Researchers found that the same areas of our brain light up in an MRI machine when we experience rejection as when we experience physical pain. That's why rejection can feel like a punch in the gut, or a knife to the heart; you're literally using the same part of the brain as when you hurt yourself physically.

The Spirit of Rejection Causes 2 Responses:

(1) Rebellion (sanguine/choleric) - opposition to one in authority or dominance
   a. open, armed, and usually unsuccessful defiance of or resistance to an established government; **b.** an instance of such defiance or resistance.

(2) Fear (melancholic/phlegmatic) – is a feeling induced by perceived danger or threat that occurs in certain types of organisms, which causes a change in metabolic and organ functions and ultimately a change in behavior, such as fleeing, hiding, or freezing from perceived traumatic events.

Notice that fear may occur from the perception of danger, which means that danger may not be present or even a factor. Your mind reacts to what it <u>thinks is real</u>, not necessarily what *is* real.

You must combat fear with **FAITH!**

Faith is the complete trust or confidence in and strong belief in God and the doctrines of the Bible, based on spiritual apprehension and acceptance rather than proof.

A MOMENT OF TRANSPARENCY FOR SINGLE PARENTS FIGHTING THE SPIRIT OF REJECTION

Years ago, when I was a recently divorced single mother of three sons, my main concern was, "Who will love me now?"

I had spent 14 years with the same man since age 21. I didn't know anything else. I thought that I only knew how to be a mother and a wife. Once the reality of divorce was inevitable, I then believed that I only really knew how to be a mother and honestly that was by default. I gave birth to children, so I had to learn mothering by trial and error.

I had forgotten that prior to having a husband and being a mother, I was actually a woman. I was a beautiful, young, gifted, intelligent, bold, adventurous, happy, vibrant woman! But at that moment in time, I felt so far away from that person that I could not fathom that she had once been me.

After a few attempted conversations and dates with some guys I realized two things. First, I was not ready for a relationship because I was still deeply hurt and traumatized by the divorce. Second, I did not LOVE MYSELF, nor did I know how to, even though it was a couple of years after my divorce. At that point, I decided that instead of concentrating on who would love me, I would learn how to love myself.

Learning to love myself was not easy at first because I didn't know what it looked like. I began to pray, read self-help books and look toward beautiful Godly examples to assist on my journey. I started by changing my eating, exercise and sleeping habits and schedules. I ensured that I took care of my hair, nails, physical dress and appearance. I would purchase small luxury items (within my budget/means) for myself (purses, shoes, jewelry) that I had always depended on my husband to gift me with. I took at least one vacation away from my children a year. On the weekends they spent with their father, I discovered new venues, restaurants and cultural entertainment within the city; yes alone! I had the time of my life! I completed my college education and I bought a house.

When I started loving myself, I no longer had a need to concentrate on who would love me.... because I DID! I even came to the realization that my heavenly father loved me most. So, you think I should have already known that? Right, me too. I did know it in theory, but I didn't know and believe it until I learned to open up to, trust, and have faith in God, His word and the Holy Spirit...with my entire life.

If I had chosen to be in a relationship with any man and marry during those years, I'm 100% positive that I would have experienced a second and possibly third divorce by now. We attract what is in us. At that time, I was depressed, broken, fearful, lacked confidence, had low self-esteem, was being tormented and consumed by the spirit-of-rejection. Imagine trying to connect with someone who had those same issues. I had nothing to give and would have been placing an impossible burden on a mere man to heal and make me whole and happy. I had to combat all of these negative emotions, the spirit-of-rejection and specifically my own self-rejection.

I mentioned in a previous chapter that I played worship and the word throughout the night to saturate my atmosphere while I slept to cast out the spirit of depression that wanted to greet me in the mornings. In addition to that strategy, I took post-it notes and wrote positive affirmations to myself on each. I posted them all over my bathroom mirror so that every time I entered my bathroom I would see and read them. I also knew that my bathroom would be my first stop every morning. I tried to read them out loud so that I could hear them in my ear gate and allow them to resonate in my psyche' and spirt. My sons saw all of my notes and I'm sure they read them, but I don't recall one of them questioning me about them. These affirmations literally helped regulate my mind and helped start my day on a positive note and in victory.

Feel free to use this concept and any of these affirmations to assist you; also make sure that you write your own:

- God has YOU on HIS MIND and the Lord Jesus LOVEs YOU!
- You are uniquely necessary for the kingdom!
- God has a PLAN and PURPOSE for your PAIN!
- You are Beautiful!
- You are intelligent!
- You are kind!
- You are DESIREABLE!
- You are becoming everything that God ordained you to be!
- You can do ALL Things Through Christ Jesus that gives you Strength!
- This TOO shall PASS!!!!!!!!!!!!!!!!!!!
- You will have whatever you say!
- You are and will continue to be a GREAT mother!
- Your every hope, dream and desire is manifesting daily!
- You are the apple of God's eye!
- You are God's choice!
- You will complete your college degree without delay or denial!
- You will receive a promotion and raise from your employer!

- God is giving you favor in every area and in everything you put your hands too!
- Your inconvenience is temporary; your sacrifice now will cause you to reap later!
- You will be a millionaire and create generational wealth.

I also began meditating on the truth of scripture and what God said about me. I am who God says I am!

Now let's get delivered from the spirit of rejection! Pray this prayer:

Father God, in the name of Jesus……. thank you for allowing me to come to you for any need that I have. I ask that you forgive me for all of my sins. Today, I make a decision that I no longer want to live with the tormenting spirit-of-rejection.
I forgive everyone who ever hurt, abused or damaged me in any way.
I forgive myself for everything I have ever done. I thank you Lord, that it is all covered under the blood of Jesus!
I come out of agreement with rejection and abandonment in Jesus' name.
I bind the strongman and uproot the spirit of rejection and any other spirits connected to it…. self-rejection, sabotage, mistrust, low-self-esteem, abandonment that tries to block my deliverance.
I proclaim that all rejection has been cast out and cut off at the cross of Jesus!
I apply the mind of Christ to my mind, the acceptance of His love and covering and total healing and deliverance in Jesus' Name!
Amen!
Now proclaim with me…. "I AM FREE!"

CHAPTER 9 - CONCENTRATING ON ME AND MY FUTURE

TAKE the attention off of the divorce, trauma and perpetrator and now concentrate on you and your future. Yes, you do have a FUTURE and it is BRIGHT!

After you have made the conscious decision to FORGIVE, there are some fundamental tools you can now put into place.

I. GIVE

Give of your time, resources, money (tithes, offerings, gifts), experiences and love. Take the focus off of your pain and situation and help somebody else.

Galatians 6:7 lets us know that, "Whatsoever a man sows that shall he also reap."

Luke 6:38 tells us to, "Give, and it will be given to

you. A good measure, pressed down, shaken together and running over, will be poured into your lap."

This may sound strange, but to keep concentrating on your pain is really being selfish. Hear me out. There is an amazing world filled with interesting people and full of amazing sights, sounds, smells and tastes waiting for you to explore, experience and be a part of. Embracing your pain causes you to miss all of these opportunities. Instead of concentrating on your pain, be intentional about helping someone else through theirs. There is always someone in a worse state or position. Go to a homeless shelter for women and children and serve for a day. I can promise you that you will see things much clearer and your pain will start to subside. As a matter of fact, this exercise in giving will cause you to see how blessed you are, and you will start giving glory to God that your situation is not as extreme. Sometimes we just need to have our lenses focused to help us through a rough emotional time.

We can't always be physically present or do the work ourselves; that's the reason there are ministries and organizations in place that we can support. When we give financially, we are partnering with the mission of our local churches or houses and extending beyond our own boarders by partnering with initiatives that we believe in and endorse.

II. SET GOALS

Set long- and short-term goals that you would like to accomplish. Write them down, post them where you can see them every day, carry them in your purse or wallet, etch them in your heart and memory then daily confess them in faith. Then check them off as God brings them to manifestation.

Habakkuk 2: 2~ "Write the vision and make it plain on tablets, that he may run who reads it."

Philippians 4:6-7~ "Do not be anxious about anything, but in every situation, by prayer and petition, with thanksgiving, present your requests to God. And the peace of God, which transcends all understanding, will guard your hearts and your minds in Christ Jesus."

This is a very delicate and vulnerable time. You are probably used to being held, holding someone and having sex even if only on occasion. It is a normal human desire to want this and love; real love. Just to be clear…these are desires. Do not confuse them with tangible goals that you set and work and progress towards accomplishing. In other words, marriage is a desire, not a goal. At this stage of the process you are not ready for emotional or any other type of romantic involvement. You are starting your healing process and do not need any distractions during this time that could cause an infection in the wound that would extend, prolong or delay your healing.

One of my short-term goals was to ensure that I took my children on vacation every year. I always believed that was one of the most important events that families could share. This was something that I didn't want to change after the divorce. Now I just had to figure a way to plan single-income family friendly vacations, and I did. Where there is a will, there is a way. I saved monthly for vacations and planned them at least 8 months to a year in advance. We started with drives to Myrtle Beach with 4 day stays in resorts, condos or timeshares and within a few years we were taking cruises to the Bahamas and flying across the states to visit and fellowship with friends. I remember my first trip alone with my sons, it was so scary. This was long before GPSs were common or popular. There was only you, the map and the road. Praise God, that our first vacation was so successful we couldn't wait to plan the next.

One of my long-term goals was to complete my bachelor's degree. Looking back on it now, I realized that it was really a short-term goal, but from my perspective at the time, it was far away. I did not get a chance to complete it before I made the decision to marry or before I became pregnant with my first child. Before there were three sons, I managed to complete my Associates (two year) degree, but in the back of my mind I always planned to go back to school after my children were older, or after my spouse completed his degree or certification in a specific skill. Neither of us lacked ambition; we just made decisions that would slow down the process of little.

When I divorced, my children were between the

ages of 5 and 13; not quite babies, but not quite independent either. Prior to the idea of divorce, I was working part-time for a consulting firm in Atlanta as a facilities manager. I knew that I would need benefits, a full paycheck and stability as a single mother; therefore, I started looking for opportunities closer to home with the package I needed. A door opened for me to contract at a federal agency and I was offered a full-time position within a few months of working there. Although I did not have any idea that I would work, grow and position myself for retirement in the agency, God knew and was ordering my steps.

From the administrative assistant's position, I could see that there was lots of opportunity at this agency. The only issue was that there was lots of opportunity for individuals with at least a bachelor's degree or higher. I felt blessed and cursed at the same time. I was now a single mom and couldn't figure out childcare or money to go back to college. I knew that I had to, or I would be stuck. I would be stuck in a place with an opportunity for future without actually having one. And then, it happened! God sent a new team leader to my office. She was a brilliant soul with a PhD in the sciences, an older lady of a different race and culture than mine. She was smart, kind and as far as I discerned did not have an ounce of prejudice in her body. She was the first person to blatantly say to me, "Kimberly, you are much too smart to be a secretary! Make a plan, go back to school and finish your degree and run this agency someday in the near future." She had a weekly 1 on 1 session with me, as she did all of the Public Health Advisors that she supervised. Every week she asked me the same question and every week I gave her the same answer for a solid 6 months. "Kimberly, have you registered for school yet?" I would respond, "No, not yet, I'm still working it out." I felt so embarrassed and became so haunted by the weekly question that I finally registered for an accelerated degree program without any idea how I would pay for it and especially who would assist with my children during my night classes. When I was not strong enough, confident enough, wise enough or convinced enough of my own value and brilliance my Heavenly Father sent someone to motivate, encourage and push me right into the path I secretly desired.

I attended classes two nights per week immediately after my eight-hour workday for over two years; and then it happened, I graduated with a Bachelor of Science in Business Administration degree!

I have now been with this same agency for 20 years with a total of 30 years government service this year 2020.

III. LIVE

Celebrate your every accomplishment in life. The fact that you woke up another day gives you another chance to accomplish a goal and a reason to celebrate. Every milestone that is reached should be celebrated.

   "Life is to be Lived" ... (Ralph Ellison)"!

John 10:10~ "The thief cometh not, but for to steal, and to kill, and to destroy: I am come that they might have life, and that they might have it more **abundantly.**"

So often I hear people say that they don't have anything to celebrate, nothing to look forward to or no reason to make a big deal out of an everyday occurrence. They don't even celebrate their own birthday! Listen, you don't have to shut down the town, but you could start learning to celebrate and live by celebrating your birthday. It doesn't have to be a party. It just needs to be a set aside event or affair that acknowledges that you entered the world and that your life is significant and does matter……especially to you!

This is a good time to try something new and different. Play and have fun. This is also a good time to remember what you like and to discover new likes! Think of the thing that you always wanted to do, but never had the chance to do. Have you thought of it? Now make a tangible plan to do it! If you've never really celebrated yourself or LIVED the concept can be a little uncomfortable and intimidating, but the only way to grow into a new normal is to be willing to be a little bit uncomfortable.

The idea is to discover who you are, what you like, what you don't like, and what you like to do without any interruptions or opinions from another party. This part of the process is crucial to your future because if you do not discover or know who you are, another person could come along and give you a false identity and narrative that you may be too vulnerable to resist.

Here are some simple ways to start...have a pampering session that includes a massage, lunch and some quiet "me" time. Attend a cultural event at a museum, attend a concert of a different genre of music than you usually listen to, attend an art exhibit, attend a play and/or a community forum. Know this, it is okay to go alone. When you are alone, you give yourself the opportunity to learn, love and appreciate your own company. Learn how to laugh, love and live out loud with yourself!

There is a BIG world just waiting for you to discover it. Start by exploring some of the suggested activities inside of your city, then explore outside of your city, then outside of your state, and before you know it, you will be ready to explore outside of the country.

COMPLETE THIS ASSIGNMENT to Help You "Concentrate on Me"

GIVING, SETTING GOALS and LIVING

(1) List three ways that you will start giving; (2) List three long term and three short term goals (Remember marriage is a desire, not a goal) and (3) List three ways that you are planning to start living:

Three Ways that I will start Giving:
1.
2.
3.

Three Short Term Goals (I will accomplish in under 1 Year):
1.
2.
3.

Three Long Term Goals I (will accomplish in 1-5 Years):
1.
2
3

Three Ways that I plan to start Living:
1.
2.
3.

CHAPTER 10 - CONTINUE HEALING AND DELIVERANCE

YOU CONTINUE the healing process daily. We are constantly in a state of being delivered. Be patient with yourself and walk out the process. If you work it; it will work!

- Give yourself time.
- Accept your feelings and know that grieving is a process.
- Be faithful and committed to church encounters, bible studies, prayer, revivals and crusades.
- Spend quality time enjoying friends and family.
- Take care of yourself. Self-care is not selfish!
- Change your lifestyle a little at a time. Start

drinking lots of water, make healthier food choices, take daily brisk walks, exercise and move your body.
- Return to your hobbies and/or explore new ones.

Notice that I did not mention that you should look for or find a new love.

As I mentioned in the previous chapter, this is a very delicate and vulnerable time. It is a normal human desire to want love, but at this stage of the process you are not ready for emotional or any other type of romantic involvement.

You are starting your healing process and do not need any distractions during this time that could cause an infection in the wound that would extend, prolong or delay your healing. Now is the time for you to focus on yourself and not another person.

WHAT TO DO WITH SEXUAL DESIRES NOW THAT YOU ARE SINGLE AGAIN:

Here is the topic that we are all really concerned or even worried about but are usually too embarrassed to talk about. Now that you are single again, what happens with your sexual and sensual desires? The real answer is NOTHING. Absolutely nothing really changes with them. If you are a normal red-blooded human being, they are still there even after you are divorced. They may even seem more intensified because you may be so used to being in a physical or sexual relationship.

One morning, after a few months, I woke up out of a peaceful sleep and there "it" was to greet me. I was on fire. I had not felt an urge or need for sex in a long time. Depression had suppressed it; therefore, my mind nor my body thought about it or processed it as a need.

I got mad! Seems like a strange response, right? I started thinking to myself that if I wasn't divorced, I would not be in this situation. I could have my husband take care of this right quick and be on my way. But, reality set in. I was there alone in my bed with "it".

I'm sure by now you understand my stance and position when it comes to my faith and spirituality, I am a born again, Bible believing, Holy Ghost filled, Jesus loving, Christian. And so, with my belief in the word of God which makes it clear that fornication or sexual intercourse outside the bonds of marriage, is a sin. Let me be clear that sex means any type of sexual intercourse or artificial stimulation outside of the bonds of marriage. Right, that includes masturbation, oral sex, or fingering.

But I was no longer married. And nothing reminded me of this truth more than that moment in my bedroom that morning. Why didn't anyone tell me about this part?! I knew that I didn't want to be a statistic or raise my sons alone. I knew that I didn't want the full responsibility of my household and that I didn't want my finances to be depleted or challenged. Of course, I knew that I wouldn't be having sex anymore, but I didn't know that I would *want* to have sex. Pain has a way of silencing all other needs or desires.

And so that dilemma began that morning. Yes, I thought about finding a boyfriend or accepting a few "booty calls"; however, in my heart I wanted to live **holy** and so I knew I had to find a way around this. So, as always, I prayed and asked the Lord to help me with this issue in the form of a husband; you know with thighs, arms, legs and other essential body parts.

What I love about the Lord is that He answers when you call! I prayed for a husband to take care of those desires, but what God sent me instead was a prayer partner. My prayer partner and I were introduced to each other by a leader at our church. She was single, never married with no children and drop-dead-gorgeous. She was what I considered the direct opposite of me. I mean, don't get me wrong, I thought I was cute but my damaged self esteem would not allow me to see myself as drop-dead-gorgeous.

I immediately tried to fathom what in the world this woman could possibly offer me as a prayer partner. I figured that she would be praying for a husband, a baby, a house and a car. But contrary to my belief, she did not pray about any of those things. She and I prayed every morning for 45 minutes before my day started with my children. She would touch and agree with me every morning not only concerning that issue, but every other issue in my life. It was a Holy-Ghost set-up!

She was a real woman of God. She had been living

holy and walking out celibacy for over a decade and wasn't quite 40 years of age then. I thought that the life she was living was virtually impossible, especially since she was so sought after by men. She introduced me to a few books and encouraged me to give my sexual desires to God rather than just waiting them out for a husband.

In addition to her being my prayer partner she also became my accountability partner. With her support and years of gaining wisdom and strategies I am happy to share with others. I am a firm believer that every process first starts with making a decision. I decided that I wanted to live holy and please God with my body. After all, according to scripture (Romans 12:1) it is my reasonable or spiritual service.

STRATEGIES FOR WALKING OUT PURITY/CELIBACY:

1. **Be careful what you allow your eyes to see and your ears to hear.** Do not entertain pornography of any sort. You should not even entertain soft pornography (people in sexy swimwear or sexy clingy dresses, lingerie or tight pants) if it causes any type of arousal in you. Do not watch movies or videos that have a sexual theme, sex scenes or overtones. Yes, that probably eliminates 90% of all movies available to you. There are

family channels, family movies, etc. that you should watch instead.

2. **Fast and Pray often.** I have found nothing that works better than fasting to relieve me of any sexual frustrations. A real fast helps to kill the flesh! By the time you push your plate away and spend time with God, the only desire you'll concentrate on for a while is food. God speaks to you and cleanses impure desires during this time.

3. **Do not spend inappropriate time alone with the opposite sex** (or either gender that you may have an attraction to). When you are weak or vulnerable, you should not spend time alone with the opposite sex even if you only consider the person your friend. I know lots of people who got pregnant by or impregnated their friend. How? Opportunity and loneliness. The two friends sitting on the sofa watching a movie can quickly turn into touching, kissing and before you know it an unplanned sexual escapade. It is best to socialize and gather in small groups. This keeps things straight. Have a meeting location and a departure location for everyone in the group.

4. **Do not talk on the phone after a decent hour (bedtime).** There is something about the darkness and the night that brings out a different spirit. It's even been noted that

symptoms of illness worsens during the night hours. Lust and perversion move about a little deeper after the sun goes down. Yes, I do know that it exists during the sunlight as well, but I've experienced the shift myself when the sun sets. The mood almost instantly changes when talking on the phone after hours and even the most innocent conversations can quickly turn to, "so what you wearing?"

5. **Date one-on-one during day hours.** There are times when a relationship needs to move to the next level where the two people only spend time together and get to experience each other on a more intimate level. Try to date during day hours. Plan daytime activities during the hours of breakfast and late lunch/early dinner. This creates the perfect atmosphere without the additional fight you can experience during darker hours. You can also see a person better in the daylight.

6. **Have an Accountability Partner.** Always remember that you are a human being. You do not have superpowers. Have an accountability/prayer partner that is stronger than you. Two people struggling with the same weakness will not make a good accountability team. You will be tripping and falling all over the place. Before you answer that booty call text or accept that midnight

movie date, call your accountability partner and be honest and transparent about what you are feeling. The right accountability partner should be able to counsel and pray you through.
7. **Have a Schedule/Itinerary**. This seems like such a simple strategy; however, it is one that really works. Assign a date and time to all of your activities on a calendar. Do not schedule a time for fornication or illegal sex. Follow your schedule and do not make provision for anyone or anything that does not align with it.
8. **Stay Busy About Your Father's Business** - Look for activities, forums and events that will afford you the opportunity to GIVE of yourself and do something for others; thus taking your attention off of you (self). If you are busy about our father's business: visiting the sick, feeding the hungry, taking care of the orphans and widows, etc. you won't have time to feed the selfish spirit of loneliness.
9. **Exercise**. When I tell you that exercise can become the best activity for your sexual frustration, know that I'm telling you the truth. It's good for your health, energy and sleep. After exercising, working all day and taking care of God's business in the evening, there will only be energy remaining for sleep.

I wish that I could tell you that during these 20 years that I have been single, that I have not had any illicit sex. Unfortunately, that is not my testimony. The reason I can give you these strategies, is because I have learned first-hand how you can get side-tracked and lose focus on your journey if these strategies are not in place. You don't have to make the same mistakes.

I had two relationships on this journey where I really thought that each of the men would be my future husband. I am still single; therefore, I don't have to tell you that they were not.

Although I have only had a couple of sexual encounters they were still detrimental to my growth, development and spiritual walk. I lost focus and many of my spiritual assignments and business opportunities were delayed and, in some cases, lost because of the distractions.

Often, we think that a sexual encounter is okay if we are in love with the person; however, being in love does not always manifest into a marriage. As a matter of fact, research shows that people that have sex/live together prior to marriage have a higher expected divorce rate than those who don't. Compromising your values can never result in the promise.

Sometimes we think that there is no one that will really want you or marry you if you do not engage in sex with them prior to marriage. It is a lie from the pit of hell. The truth is that most sexual relationships do not transition into marriage. Think of how many sexual relationships you have had. How many marriages resulted from them? Be honest, you expected the sex to woo the person to the altar. No, not just the sex, but certainly you thought that the sex would help get your there. And it didn't!

Yes, you can abstain from sex until marriage. I have known multiple couples that have abstained until marriage and couples who are presently abstaining until their wedding day.

I am happy to inform you that if you are in a sexual relationship with someone you are not married to that you can stop and be delivered. What I love about God is that He wipes our slates clean and gives us a brand new start at any point and stage in our lives that we submit our will and lives to Him.

God has kept me sexually pure for many years now. I am worth the wait until marriage and so are you!

Family, this process has not been seamless. I have made a few mistakes along the way, but one thing I am convinced of is that God does not waste any pain. He uses it on our journeys. It is the foundation of our compassion and drive to ease the burdens of those who follow the same paths behind us.

I literally would not give anything for this journey. I would not trade the pain, suffering or sacrifice for anything I can think of on earth. The divorce was a part of the plan for my life's work and assignment. I am honored and humbled that my Heavenly Father chose and entrusted me to clear a path for many of His sons and daughters that would have to travel this way.

I am the happiest that I have ever been in my life and it keeps getting better every day.

Yes, there is LIFE After Divorce and **after the rip.**

ABOUT THE AUTHOR

KIMBERLY ELAINE ADAMS is the first born of five children to her parents and the first grandchild born on both sides of her family. She is the mother of 3 adult sons and is a grandmother.

She is proud to be a veteran of the United States Army and has been employed with the US Federal Government for over 30 years. Her public health career offers her the opportunity to travel internationally where she has been blessed to visit over 34 countries within the continents of Africa, Europe and Asia.

Kimberly is a daughter of The Harvest Tabernacle Church under the leadership of Apostle Travis Jennings and Pastor Stephanie Jennings where she has served in ministry for over 14 years. She was ordained and commissioned as a Minister of the gospel in 2016.

She presently serves as the Maximizing Life Singles

Ministry leader for 10 years and is presently the Life After Divorce (LAD) Support Group facilitator.

She has a profound Love for singles! She believes that all of her life experiences including the trauma of divorce was designed to develop her to be a beacon of wisdom and healing for others.

Kimberly received her Bachelors of Science in Business Administration from Shorter University, Rome, GA.

Connect with Kimberly Elaine Adams on social media.

Facebook: MsKimberlyEAdams1
Instagram: mskimberlyeadams
Website: MsKimberlyEAdams.com

www.ingramcontent.com/pod-product-compliance
Lightning Source LLC
Chambersburg PA
CBHW070510100426
42743CB00010B/1797